"Trinity's writing is gorgeously fresh. . . . This beautiful book bursts with care and advice well worth following."

—Tamar Adler, author of *An Everlasting Meal*

"Precisely the type of cookbook I crave to read these days. It is proof that good taste still matters—in all senses of the word."

—Fanny Singer, author of *Always Home: A Daughter's Recipes & Stories*

"Trinity makes a convincing case that peace and delight can be found right at our fingertips—in the sanctuaries of our home kitchens. You'll find great recipes in *Eating at Home*, yes. If you're like me, you'll also find nourishment of the spiritual variety."

—Jeff Gordinier, food and drinks editor at *Esquire*

"*Eating at Home* is a hug of a cookbook—equal parts joy, flavor, and heart. Trinity's recipes remind us that home cooking is where the good stuff happens."

—Christina Tosi, chef and founder of Milk Bar

POMODORI PELA

Trinity Mouzon Wofford
with Rebecca Firkser

EATING at HOME

The Nourishing Practice of Everyday Cooking

Photography by Dane Tashima
Illustrations by Issey Kobori

TEN SPEED PRESS
California | New York

For Ruby and Maia

WECK

CONTENTS

INTRODUCTION

This is a book of my family's meals. It will tell you all about our groceries, which cutting boards we like, and how to roast a chicken for dinner on a weeknight. The recipes that follow are some of my greatest treasures, and I believe they will change your cooking for the better. But I didn't write this book to tell you how to make dinner. I wrote this book because of what everyday cooking really feeds us with: connection.

The last three years of writing this book have granted me the opportunity to reflect on how my family comes together for a meal. Most of our quality time revolves around food—hitting the local markets, tending to a pot of stock, or sitting around the table. Making a record of our rituals led me to a question I'd been circling: What makes from-scratch cooking worth the time and attention it asks of us?

When we enjoy food that's been simply prepared with quality ingredients, we're benefitting from a more nutritious meal than anything that comes in a package, no matter what the glossy labels might suggest. Cooking is also the quiet champion of household economics, often far more cost-effective than dining out or relying on a rotation of prepared foods.

But as I've stacked the layers on my daughter's berries-and-cream birthday cake, or paused for lunch in the face of a mind-withering to-do list, I've found that health and budget can't quite summarize the source of my dedication.

In equal measure, this book is about our meals and our moments. Through the process of bringing this book to fruition, I've been writing, mothering, recipe testing, running our family business, and recipe testing again. Life has been gorgeously and overwhelmingly full. Through all of it, we've been sitting down at our table to eat.

My practice of home cooking began ten years ago, while my husband, Issey, and I were living in Brooklyn and had just started Golde, our natural wellness business. In the early days, we weren't taking salaries and instead pulled forty dollars a week out of our checking account to cover our groceries. I quickly noticed that our dollars went furthest at the local farmers' market. As seasons passed, I learned to look beyond the ephemeral strawberries to the hardworking root vegetables and greens that would form the foundation of our meals. I discovered that shiitake and oyster mushrooms could sub in for the richness of meat at a fraction of the cost.

Every Saturday morning, we lugged our Greenmarket haul from Union Square back to our apartment in Bed-Stuy. At home in our kitchen, we let the ingredients lead the way. September's carrots were roasted with olive oil and salt and served with a three-ingredient yogurt and dill sauce. On the days I most deeply resented living in a fourth-floor walk-up with absolutely no air-conditioning, July's cucumbers and tomatoes were sliced and tossed with vinegar and cold buckwheat noodles for a soothing plate of relief. In the dead of winter, we pulled pickled red cabbage from the fridge and enjoyed it over rice. (Almost everything was over rice, partly due to Issey's Japanese heritage, but also because there is no simpler and more cost-effective way to fill your belly.)

As I fell into the rhythms of eating at home, I found that this daily ritual did more than manage my shoestring budget. Cooking balanced my busy days with pause, something I so desperately needed in my entrepreneurial frenzy.

Many years have passed since those humble beginnings: Issey and I now live in a creaking old house in upstate New York with our two girls, about an hour from our shared hometown. The practice of eating well at home remains a constant. We make the majority of our food from scratch, largely with ingredients that we can trace back to a local producer. We sit down to eat at the table in the company of whoever is around, even if it's a 10-minute jam-and-toast breakfast before the day begins.

A cooking practice asks that we trade in some of our efficiencies for attention—noticing where our food comes from, being present as we cook, and sitting down to truly pause for a meal. But like a tiny seed just watered in a garden, the yield is infinite in comparison to the efforts put in. A tiny shift now becomes a reclamation: of our time, our nourishment, and our sense of connection to the people we break bread with.

So much of our food culture today relies on hacks and tricks to get around the task of cooking and eating. Our mealtimes are hurried so that we can get on to the next thing. But a good practice isn't centered on outcomes—with each vegetable we chop or pot we stir, we are humbly reminded of the merits of the present moment.

This book is organized to make a cooking practice delightfully possible. In chapter 1, we'll learn how to bring better ingredients home without abandoning our budgets. Next, we'll build a practice of Component Cooking, my answer to meal-prep that makes from-scratch food an everyday reality. The rest of the book walks you through our moments together at home by chapter, from weeknight-friendly dinners to Sunday morning's sourdough pancakes. Each recipe is grounded in easy techniques and nourishing ingredients that will make home cooking a grounding rhythm in your daily life.

I believe the simple act of cooking and eating at home will help you be more present with yourself and in the shared moments with the people you love. Together, we'll learn that good-quality, simple food *is* health food—and that the ingredients you cook with are as important as the gentleness you bring to the process.

We're all strapped for time, and sometimes it feels like even the act of eating itself is conspiring against our heaving to-do lists. Short of committing to an all-liquid diet, I'd like to suggest a radical alternative: Make space for food. Let the shopping, cooking, and sitting at the table for mealtime be the restorative part of your day. Let eating at home be the thing that we've been missing—a willingness to enjoy the process will make it something to savor. The day will still be there when we put our forks down.

In today's world, the home tends not to be as productive a place as it once was. We take jobs elsewhere, earn money, buy things and bring them home to use. If we want our families to benefit from work undertaken together, we have deliberately to set up situations where that can happen . . . Breadbaking maybe, or a vegetable garden, the tasks assigned by age and skill.

—*Laurel Robertson,* The Laurel's Kitchen Bread Book

WHAT NOURISHES US

(A Primer on Eating Well)

I abide by three pillars of eating well: filling the kitchen with wholesome ingredients, mastering a few beginner-friendly techniques, and maintaining a willingness to enjoy the process. The mission of this book is to get you to embrace the possibilities of each.

I'll put it simply: Ingredients matter. The quality and freshness of what you're cooking with will have a tremendous influence on how easily you can whip up something that tastes *really* good. I know that we've all grown accustomed to the convenience of supermarkets and grocery-delivery apps, but I'm going to make the case that being a little more intentional with your shopping will pay off in dividends when you get into the kitchen.

Not all apples are created equal. We've witnessed a dramatic decrease in the nutrient quality of our fruits and vegetables in just the last sixty years. This is largely due to the rise of intensive, commercial-scale farming that produces bigger, more dependable yields at the cost of quality. Common produce like bananas, tomatoes, and oranges have lost 25 to 50 percent of their nutritional density since 1950. Fresh produce in the United States now travels an average of 1,500 miles before being consumed, and nutrients from vitamin C to folate have been shown to rapidly decline with every passing day between harvest and consumption.

When we get our fresh vegetables and fruits from commercial suppliers at big-box supermarkets, we're unknowingly buying into a system that's responsible for our own declining access to nutritious foods.

The good news is that buying from local producers can greatly increase the nutritional value, flavor, and sustainability impact of the foods you love to eat. The farm-to-table movement has created increasing demand for local, in-season produce, which means you can now find it everywhere, from your weekly farmers' market to your nearest grocery store.

The preparation of food also serves the soul in a number of ways. In a general sense, it gives us a valuable, ordinary opportunity to meditate quietly, as we peel and cut vegetables, stir pots, measure out proportions, and watch for boiling and roasting.

—*Thomas Moore,* The Re-Enchantment of Everyday Life

FOOD SHOPPING MAKES A VILLAGE

Every Saturday, I make a ritual of visiting the farmers' market with my family. It functions as our grocery shopping, but it also feeds us with community. It would certainly be easier to get groceries delivered to my door, but I believe there's value in stepping out into the world and meeting with our local growers and neighbors. With two small children, we also see it as a weekly opportunity to connect them to our "village." Many of the vendors know our daughters by name and have watched them grow over the years. As we search for our lettuces and cucumbers, my elder daughter wields a small grocery tote to carry her whole-grain croissant from a local baker. We run into friends and enjoy the casual joy of catching up in between our errands. By shopping directly with the farmers, we've prioritized putting our dollars directly toward supporting their operations, rather than an industrial system that pays out to distributors, transporters, and supermarket stocking fees.

By loading up on high-quality produce, we've effectively simplified the cooking process. I once heard from a chef who worked in high-end, European kitchens that fruits and vegetables are perfect as they are. The goal when preparing them is to do as little as possible, to simply enhance their beautiful flavors and textures. This is the ethos I cook by. Assembling a gorgeous plate of food is about celebrating the stuff in my hands, rather than trying to transform it with lengthy, complicated techniques.

Beyond the world of fruits and veg, there's a lot of value to being intentional with the rest of your shopping list, too. Everything from eggs to olive oil will benefit immensely from thoughtful sourcing, but with the prices we're seeing today, it's fair to wonder if you've been priced out of access to good-quality food altogether. Fortunately, when you compare the costs of packaged foods and takeout, a meal that's made from scratch will almost always save money. You'll probably spend more on a quart of local cows' milk than the national brand equivalent—but start where you can. Inspiring yourself to eat more home-cooked meals by beginning with delicious, nourishing ingredients will pay off in more ways than one.

Where to Shop

I will advocate that the most important decision you can make about your food is where it comes from. Produce, grains, dairy, and meat will all be of much higher quality when they come from a smaller producer that's close to home. The better ingredients you're working with, the less you have to do with them. A bit of intentionality in your shopping will go a tremendous way in letting your cooking practice be easy and inspired.

Farmers' Markets

Farmers' markets have become seasonal standards in many American cities and towns. Make a habit of visiting yours each week. You'll learn about what's in season at different points in the year and build relationships with the growers themselves. To find a market near you, check your state's agricultural resources for a directory—or ask a friend who loves to cook.

Farm CSAs

CSA stands for "community supported agriculture," where you can purchase a seasonal share with a local farm. In exchange for guaranteeing income for the farm up front, you can pick up a box full of produce every week for the next couple of months. In larger cities, I have seen farms set up pick-up locations at small businesses or even deliver to home addresses. The farms decide what's in the box, so this is a great option if you prefer not to have to make decisions about what to buy.

Food Co-ops

Food cooperatives are grocery stores collectively owned by their members. Each co-op is a little different, but members will typically get discounts in exchange for the one-time purchase of an owner's share. Thanks to the focus on local suppliers, it's estimated that every dollar spent at a food co-op generates $1.60 for the local economy. (Many co-ops allow nonmembers to shop there, too—give your local one a call to find out.)

Natural Foods Stores

Natural foods stores are typically smaller operations than supermarkets. They can provide a lot of the same value and merchandise as food co-ops, focusing on local producers and higher-quality ingredients than larger supermarkets.

Supermarkets

Supermarkets offer maximum convenience but the least value for your dollar in terms of nutritious, locally produced food. Fortunately, consumer demand is shaping what we find in the aisles—look for signs highlighting local suppliers, opting for those whenever you can.

SEASONAL EATING (AND WHEN IT REALLY MATTERS)

Eating "in season" means consuming produce that was grown at the time it naturally grows. Fruits, roots, and leaves all develop at different times in a plant's life cycle, and eating alongside nature's tempo has many upsides.

It's possible to grow fruit outside of its proper season (you see strawberries at the supermarket year-round), but at the cost of flavor and nutrients. When we eat the berry that was grown in June instead of January, we're greatly reducing the number of commercial resources that were involved in producing it. The result is a more efficient path to what we really want: very simple, very wholesome, and very delicious food.

In a perfect world, we'd all only eat what was grown within a hundred-mile radius of our homes. Food that's freshly picked will *always* beat out the commercially grown produce in flavor and texture (not to mention those pesky disappearing nutrients). Getting started with small changes can make a difference—don't get hung up on perfection.

For the easiest way to eat seasonally, find your local farmers' market or farm CSA. If they've got it, it's in season.

We've forgotten today to wait for seasonal delicacies, and as a punishment, the grocery store has become a year-round warehouse of indifferent fruit and vegetable staples.

—*Kevin West,* Saving the Season

Supplement Facts
ORGANIC INDIA
cook book

FOUNDATIONAL INGREDIENTS

Here's the thing: No amount of cooking know-how will make up for low-quality ingredients. A lot of what's on the supermarket shelves is not produced with care, which nets out to worse flavor and nutrition. Fortunately, "the good stuff" can be found within reach and within budget, with a little extra attention to sourcing.

A Produce "Pantry"

I treat my fresh produce like pantry staples, stocking up on the essentials that are available nearly year-round. You'll see root vegetables and hearty greens repeated often. By keeping the same things on hand, I'm rarely caught in the "what can I cook with this" paralysis.

Salt

I keep three salts around. Fine and coarse sea salts are both stored in glass jars by the stovetop for easy access while cooking. Fine salt blends into other ingredients more easily, while coarse salt has more texture. A little dish of flaky sea salt sits at the table for sprinkling on top of just about everything. I never use iodized table salt: It doesn't taste as good, can contain anticaking agents, and is very salty by volume, which means it's easy to oversalt when using it to cook.

Which Brand of Salt Is Best?

Every salt will be unique in its degree of saltiness by volume, so you'll want to get comfortable knowing how to salt your meals to taste with what you've got on hand. I recommend sea salt, which is rich in minerals that will add a savory depth of flavor to your food, not just saltiness. I use Gucciardo Trapani fine sea salt most often for cooking and baking, which I order in 2-pound bags for less than $5.

Olive Oil

A grassy, fresh-pressed olive oil will transform your simplest dishes. I don't subscribe to the theory of saving your "good" olive oil for precious garnishing. Find an extra-virgin olive oil that fits your budget and use it liberally in all your cooking projects, even baking.

Note: Look for olive oil that prints a harvest date and ideally was sourced from a single grower. It doesn't age nicely like a bottle of wine, so don't be too precious: Use it within 3 months once opened. If your olive oil smells waxy, it's already sat in your pantry (or supermarket's shelf) for too long.

Rice

I keep two types of rice on hand: a short-grain Japanese rice and a longer-grain, American-grown rice. I love the taste and texture of white rice, so instead of fiber-rich brown rice I prefer to get the extra nutrients from whatever I serve alongside.

Milk, Butter, and Yogurt

Don't fear the fat: I cook with whole-fat milk, butter, and yogurt. The fats in these whole foods will help to keep you fuller for longer and may make it easier to absorb the critical fat-soluble vitamins (A, D, E, and K) in other ingredients. Cream-top milk is the best thing to look for at your local grocery, because it means that the milk is unhomogenized (homogenization is an unnecessary process that breaks up milk fat particles to yield a uniform texture). I buy Amish-style butter that comes in a large roll—it's more cost effective than buying sticks. Whole-milk yogurt is great as the main event for breakfast, but I also love to have it on hand for whipping up creamy sauces, softening the spice of a curried stew, and lending tangy richness to baked goods. I prefer Greek-style yogurts because they're thicker in texture and not too sour.

Eggs

Fresh eggs will have bright yellow or orange yolks, and the whites will be viscous, not watery. Unfortunately, popular labels like "cage-free" don't mean a whole lot when it comes to animal welfare or the quality of the eggs themselves. "Free range" or "pasture-raised" implies that the chickens have some access to the outdoors, which is a slight improvement. The best eggs will always come from a smaller farm that's local to you. Look for a single source listed on the carton, rather than a larger brand that aggregates eggs from hundreds of farms. To test if the eggs you're getting are fresh, submerge them in cold water. Fresh eggs will lie horizontally and sink to the bottom, while older eggs (which absorb air over time) will stand upright and eventually float all the way to the top of the water.

Spices and Dried Herbs

I always try to buy spices in their whole form instead of preground, because the flavor is much fresher. Try cooking with whole seeds if they're very small (like fennel or cumin). Coriander seed is similar in size to peppercorns and can either be roughly crushed with the back of a spoon or (my favorite) ground fresh in a pepper mill.

I'm not too prescriptive when it comes to exactly which spices and dried herbs to stock, because the best thing to do is develop your own favorites as you keep cooking. Here's what I like to keep on hand:

- Bay leaves
- Black peppercorns
- Ground cinnamon
- Coriander seeds
- Fennel seeds
- Granulated garlic or garlic powder
- Whole nutmeg
- Sage leaves
- Sesame seeds (try toasting, page 67, for more flavor)
- Shiso

Fresh Herbs

I like to keep a bunch of fresh parsley in a cup of water, like a leafy bouquet. It will last a few days on the countertop, and a little longer in the refrigerator. Fresh tender herbs like parsley, cilantro, dill, shiso, and tarragon add bright freshness to dishes. Sprigs of fresh woody herbs like oregano, thyme, rosemary,

marjoram, and sage add depth to brothy beans and fragrance to roast chicken. Scallions are technically a vegetable, but I use them often, much as I do fresh tender herbs: raw and thinly sliced to finish a dish.

Nuts and Seeds

A handful of chopped nuts is one of the easiest ways to complete a meal. Walnuts, hazelnuts, and sesame seeds appear on my family's table daily. They add wonderful flavor and texture to food, and are rich in fat, fiber, and protein.

Flour and Other Grains

Using gently processed flour made from higher-quality grains can sometimes make all the difference in how easy it is to digest bread and other gluten-rich baked goods. I rely on unbleached all-purpose and whole wheat flour for baking. Sometimes I'll mix in rye to lend a denser texture and a nuttier flavor. Earthy buckwheat flour, cornmeal (stone-ground and polenta), and oats (steel-cut for eating, rolled for baking) are also always in my pantry. Store grains in the freezer if you have room, especially if you use them infrequently. They'll keep fresh for much longer, and you'll taste the difference.

Sweeteners

I cook with so much maple syrup. Friends laugh when they open my refrigerator to see a 5-gallon jug front and center, but I've got my reasons. Maple is low-glycemic, so it doesn't spike your blood sugar in the same way sugar or honey would. I do use unbleached granulated cane sugar and raw local honey in moderation. Most sweet recipes can use far less sugar and still taste perfectly balanced.

Fish

I like cooking whole fish, like mackerel, sardines, or red snapper—it's usually much more economical than buying fillets. Fresh clams feel elegant (and cook so easily) but can usually be found for a very reasonable price. Tinned fish, like oil-packed tuna, is a great lunch protein to keep on hand.

Thoughtfully Sourced Meat

The matter of sourcing is especially important when we're talking about animal products. Unfortunately, regulation standards in the United States can allow for the excess use of growth hormones and antibiotics, inhumane crowding, and other troublesome production methods. Each of these negatively impact the nutritional value, environmental integrity, and (of course) flavor of what you're eating. Because meat isn't an everyday thing in my home, I prefer to be smart about where I'm getting it from and how it was raised. I look for local producers at my grocery store or visit the vendors directly at the weekend farmers' market. Farmers' market meat is often frozen, so if you're looking to cook it the same day, account for thawing time: about 24 hours in the fridge, or submerged in the packaging, in a bowl of cold water, changed out every 30 minutes for a few hours, until defrosted.

BUY IN BULK

If you want to dramatically increase the value of your dollar at the grocery store, buy in bulk. As prices continue to rise with inflation (and my family continues to grow), I've learned how to source nearly every one of our pantry staples in bulk for a savings. For example, I order olive oil in 9-liter jugs from a supplier in California and decant it into a smaller glass bottle to use while cooking. Maple syrup is much more economical by the gallon than those pretty little bottles, too. If you bake with any frequency, seek out flour in 10-pound bags or more. (I get fresh, locally milled flour for a cheaper rate than the supermarket standards simply by buying more at a time.) Salt, dried beans, spices, and even peanut butter are all worth buying in bulk. You'll save yourself the cost of all that extra packaging, which makes a big difference in your grocery bills. Thanks to the internet, it's never been easier to buy direct from independent producers of great quality. A local food co-op or natural foods store will also likely have a bulk section that stocks many of your grocery essentials. I've even had my local store special-order the flour they stock in a larger size for me to pick up—no shipping charge. You may be able to earn a discount this way (I've gotten up to 20 percent off my bill). If a bulk quantity is more than you can use in a reasonable time, consider splitting a large order with friends or neighbors. My goal is always to get the simplest, highest quality (nutritious and delicious) food for my family: Buying in bulk makes it affordable and low-waste.

TRADES AND SWAPS

We can't beat the power of the almighty dollar. But as you start making your own fresh food from scratch, try experimenting with the age-old tradition of swapping goods with a friend. Most recently, Issey and I traded a day's farm work for a Thanksgiving turkey, and fresh sourdough bread for our neighbor's homegrown raspberry jam. You don't need to go into full-scale bartering mode, but trading within your community is deeply rewarding. Your biscuits for my pickles. My garden tomatoes for your garden cannabis. You get it.

GOOD OLD-FASHIONED TOOLS

When it comes to kitchen gadgets, I am enthusiastically low-fi (with a few exceptions). There will always be a shiny new appliance that promises to revolutionize the way you cook, but I don't buy it. I believe in cooking good, simple food—the kind of meals that need little more than a cutting board and frying pan.

I do my absolute best to avoid plastic kitchen tools and I never use nonstick pans. Look for items made from iron, wood, and stainless steel that could have belonged to your grandmother: These are the hardworking essentials that will last a lifetime, not a season.

Knives

If you haven't sharpened your knives recently, they are already dull. A sharp knife cuts effortlessly, making prep work fast, enjoyable, and much safer. Lately I'm seeing more local services popping up for knife-sharpening, but you can also do it yourself quite easily. Skip the electric sharpening gadgets and buy a whetstone—it's a one-time investment that will last you for years to come. Take a few minutes to sharpen your knives every couple of months, or whenever you notice they aren't moving through your prep as gracefully as you'd like.

A Wooden Cutting Board

A wooden cutting board is easier on your knife (the blade won't dull as quickly) and won't inadvertently shed plastic fibers into everything you eat. I have one small cutting board set aside for fruits and mild-flavored veg, which prevents my apple slices from picking up an undertone of yesterday's crushed garlic. Wooden cutting boards should be gently washed by hand and reoiled regularly (I use a few drops of olive oil). Keeping your cutting boards oiled will also prevent them from picking up food odors over time, so don't skip this step.

Iron Pots and Pans

Traditional cast-iron, carbon steel, and stainless steel pans are superior to the new wave of nonstick technology. Brand-new cast-iron and carbon steel pans may need to be seasoned before you start cooking with them. I like Lodge for cast-iron and de Buyer or Mauviel for carbon steel. I also use enameled cast-iron Dutch ovens (Staub is my favorite manufacturer; 6 quarts is a good size to start with), which do not require any seasoning. Avoid using metal utensils with these, which can scratch the coating. This kind of classic cookware requires a little bit of getting used to, but the simple technique of making sure your pan is properly heated before adding oil (and that the oil is hot before adding anything else) will prevent any food from sticking—no chemical coatings required.

A Spice Mill

I like to fill a pepper grinder with other dried spices. Whole coriander seeds add a floral, citrusy note when cracked over pastas, soups, and salads. I find that keeping my favorite seasonings on hand this way makes me much more apt to use them in my everyday cooking.

The Only Appliances

A good kitchen scale is essential. This makes more exact recipes, like baking or fermenting pickles, truly foolproof. I also keep a rice cooker, coffee grinder, and my Vitamix blender nearby. A handheld immersion blender is helpful when I don't want to use the Vitamix. I don't bother with recipes that require a stand mixer, but you can use one instead of a whisk to beat batters as desired.

One Last Thing

I couldn't conclude a section on the tools of my kitchen without a small love note to my special ceramic tea cups, the wooden spoon my husband carved for me, or the antique plates passed down from my grandmother. Let your kitchen be an extension of what makes you feel at home. Invest in the small treasures that make your cooking and eating routine joyful. If you've got an old, chipped cutting board that makes you heave a heavy sigh every time you use it, just replace it already. Cooking is an opportunity to enjoy the moment—go ahead and try it.

USING AND CARING FOR IRON PANS

Cast-iron and carbon steel pans' nonstick qualities improve the more they're cooked in. To avoid sticking, use them often and don't skimp on the cooking fat. These pans don't need to be washed with soap. To clean, wipe off any excess grease with hot water and a sponge. Heat on low on your stovetop to dry off excess moisture. To avoid rusting, wipe down with a little oil. Allow to cool and store as usual.

COMPONENT

COOKING

Every Sunday, I set aside some time to blanch whatever vegetables are on hand from my most recent trip to the local farmers' market, boil grains, roast a pot full of sweet potatoes, or simmer leftover chicken and vegetable scraps into a rich, golden broth. I'll transfer everything to containers in the fridge, where they will eventually become elements of various meals throughout the coming days. This practice keeps me ready for the workweek, when "What's for dinner?" is not always a question I'm willing to answer with grace. I like to call it Component Cooking.

Don't think of this as harried meal prep; with Component-Cooked elements, putting together a meal in the moment becomes a breezy assembly. The recipes in this chapter are unhurried, and the techniques are easy and forgiving. You can take a look ahead to the next chapters to see how these components come together for breakfast, lunch, and dinner. Getting some inspiration with finished dishes will help you to decide what to Component Cook on a slower-paced day. With a well-stocked fridge of foundational foods, the only task ahead is to decide whether you'd like those beans with rice or pasta, which herbs and seasonings would be delicious additions to transform that pot of stock into a simple soup, and whether to add a hefty slice of buttered bread to the side (the answer is yes). Relax, enjoy, you did it with ease—that's how cooking can be.

$0 SCRAP STOCK

Makes about 2 quarts

In my home, a good stock is the foundation of nourishing meals. The backbone of this stock recipe is salvaged cooking scraps (onion trimmings, carrot stems, chicken bones, and the like), which makes it essentially free. Throughout the week, I collect cooking scraps and store them in the freezer in a gallon-size bag.

A warning: Once you start making stock yourself, all store-bought varieties will pale in comparison (you will also pale at the price tag). The cooking itself takes time but is outrageously simple and mostly hands-off. A big batch can be distributed into 1-quart containers and stowed in the freezer. I take a container out every week for flavoring brothy pastas, cooking grains, and, of course, creating a base for a great soup.

Gluten-free, vegan option

---

3 pounds (about one full 1-gallon zip-top bag) vegetable scraps (see Which Scraps for Stock?, page 36), fresh or frozen

2 chicken carcasses, or 3 pounds chicken bone scraps, fresh or frozen

2 dried bay leaves

2 tablespoons black peppercorns

1 tablespoon apple cider vinegar

2 teaspoons fennel or coriander seeds (optional)

2 medium onions (optional), quartered

3 carrots (optional), scrubbed and quartered

Sea salt

NOTE: For vegan stock, skip the chicken and double the amount of veg scraps (skip the vinegar).

If using frozen scraps: Preheat the oven to 425°F.

Divide the frozen vegetable and chicken scraps between two sheet pans. Roast until everything is thawed, aromatic, and just beginning to caramelize, about 20 minutes. (If you're using nonfrozen veg, this step is optional, but still adds a richer flavor to your finished stock.) Pour ½ cup water onto the sheet pan and use a spatula to scrape up any caramelized bits.

For the stock: Add the scraps (roasted or unroasted) to the biggest pot you have (at least 6 quarts or two smaller ones).

Add the bay leaves, peppercorns, vinegar, fennel seeds (if using), and fresh onions and/or carrots (if using). Add at least 10 cups of water, until the solids are mostly covered, going up to the top of the pot(s) as needed.

Bring to a boil over medium-high heat. Reduce the heat to low and simmer, partially covered, until the liquid is deeply golden in color, 1 to 2 hours. Turn off the heat.

Let the stock cool for about 10 minutes. Use tongs to remove and discard the solids from the pot, then strain into a large bowl. Stir in a couple pinches of salt.

Transfer the stock to airtight containers. Refrigerate for up to 4 days; or cool completely in the fridge, then freeze for up to 6 months.

WHICH SCRAPS FOR STOCK?

Stock is made by slowly simmering vegetables and/or meat bones until they release their rich flavor and nutrients into the cooking water. Use the good-quality odds and ends of the produce you're already eating. Frozen scraps keep well in the freezer for up to 6 months.

VEG

Celery, carrot, onion, scallion, leeks, mushroom, sweet corn cob, sweet pepper, tomato. Peeled skins are great; wilted or bruised veg is fine. Starting to mold or rot? Send it to the compost bin (see opposite page). Make sure any dirt is rinsed from vegetable trimmings before storing.

MEAT BONES AND OTHER SCRAPS

Leftover beef, chicken, and pork bones, relatively cleaned of meat (this is a great use for what's left of a roast chicken or bone-in steak). If you have them, try old-school scrappy cuts like chicken necks or feet, and beef soup bones, which are usually available for cheap from a butcher's counter.

I always add 1 tablespoon apple cider vinegar to help extract collagen and minerals from the bones, which yields the richest stock. Don't add any vinegar if you're just using vegetables, as it can make the whole batch a bit sour.

AVOID USING

Brassicas like kale, broccoli, and cabbage (a handful or two is okay, but a lot will turn your stock bitter); any trimmings that are too dirt-caked to rinse completely clean.

IN SMALL QUANTITIES

Half a lemon, a few chunks of ginger, Parmesan cheese rinds, handfuls of apple peels, woody herbs like sage, oregano, or thyme can add flavor without overpowering the stock.

Variations

Corn Cob Stock

Sub 4 **pounds (about 5) corn cobs** (no need to roast in advance) for the veg and meat scraps to make a mild, sweet stock that's great for soups like Fennel, Corn, and Clam Chowder (page 173).

Scallion Trimmings Stock

Swap the veg scraps with the washed ends (root and any unused dark green tops) of **2 to 3 pounds of scallions** (leek, chive, and spring onion trimmings work great here, too) with a peeled **knob of ginger** (about the size of two thumbs) for a fragrant and slightly sweet stock. I also like using **pork scraps** in addition to or instead of chicken in this stock. It's great in Japanese-style dishes like Steaming Miso Nabe (page 178) and Soothing Rice Porridge (page 95).

PUT IT TO USE

Broth-Simmered Farro (page 48)
Curried Lentil Stew (page 132)
Sheet Pan Kabocha-Ginger Soup (page 145)
"Instant" Any-Veg Soup (page 133)
Fall-Apart Braised Beef Shanks (page 177)
Braised Collards with Smoky Shiitake (page 181)

MAKE COMPOST

Beyond making $0 Scrap Stock (page 34), composting is one of the best ways to reduce food waste. Compost is a natural fertilizer that looks like a rich, dark garden soil. It's made when organic material (like your eggshells, coffee grounds, and banana peels) break down with the help of soil microorganisms. Right now, the vast majority of our food waste is sent to landfills, where an anaerobic decomposition process releases harmful greenhouse gases into the atmosphere. When compost is added to soil as a fertilizer, on the other hand, it acts like a multivitamin for our crops. It also ensures that we can grow nutrient-rich produce with higher yields, less water waste, and fewer commercial pesticides.

Wherever you live, you have options beyond sending your food scraps to a landfill. As a home gardener, I keep a compost pile in my backyard. Over time, a mix of food scraps, leaves, and grass clippings transforms into a zero-waste organic fertilizer for my plants. If you live in a more urban area, many cities now run their own municipal compost programs with curbside pick-up bins or drop-off locations. You can also find a neighbor or a community garden that will happily accept your compostables.

60:40 BEANS

Makes about 7 cups beans, plus broth; serves 6 to 8

The secret to a great pot of beans is the vegetables you cook them with. I use a rough ratio of 40 percent dried beans to 60 percent aromatic vegetables, like onion, celery, fennel, and carrot. The veg adds dimension via texture and flavor to mild beans, making the finished product a ready-made base for soups and brothy pastas, but is just as good over rice or with a piece of grilled bread.

Gluten-free, vegan

---

1 pound (about 2 cups) preferred dried beans (see Which Beans? page 41)

One 3-inch piece kombu, lightly crushed (optional; see Note)

¼ cup extra-virgin olive oil

2 tablespoons fennel seeds (optional)

1 tablespoon coriander seeds

4 garlic cloves, smashed and peeled

1 large red or yellow onion, coarsely chopped

3 large celery stalks, coarsely chopped

2 medium carrots, scrubbed and coarsely chopped

1 dried bay leaf

½ bunch fresh herbs (optional)

Sea salt

Place the beans in a colander and rinse thoroughly.

Transfer the beans to a large bowl with the kombu (if using). Pour water into the bowl until the beans are covered by 3 inches. Let the beans soak for at least 6 or up to 12 hours.

Drain the soaked beans, rinse thoroughly, and set aside.

In a large heavy-bottom pot, heat the oil over medium heat. Add the fennel and coriander seeds (if using) and toast, stirring often, until fragrant, about 1 minute. Stir in the drained beans, garlic, onion, celery, carrots, bay leaf, fresh herbs (if using), and a couple big pinches of salt. Add water to cover the beans by at least 2 inches.

Increase the heat to high and bring the mixture to a boil, skimming off any foam from the surface. Reduce to medium-low, partially cover, and cook, stirring very occasionally, and adding water as needed to keep the beans covered, until the beans are tender. Beans will take 1 to 2 hours to cook through, depending on the variety. Season with more salt to taste.

Remove from the heat and serve immediately. If reserving for later use, cool the beans for 10 minutes. Transfer to airtight containers and let cool to warm room temperature.

Store the beans in the refrigerator for up to 1 week, or in the freezer (best in 1-quart containers for easy thawing) for up to 6 months.

NOTE: Kombu is dried Japanese seaweed. I like to simmer a piece with the beans, as the natural enzymes in the kombu help to make the beans easier to digest. (I crush the dried seaweed into little pieces with my hands before adding it to the beans, which dissolve into the broth as the mixture cooks—and no, you won't taste it.) You can find kombu among other Asian grocery staples at the supermarket, but you can also still enjoy this recipe without it.

Variations

Simple Garlic Chickpeas

While you can use chickpeas with the 60:40 bean-to-veg method on page 38, sometimes simple is best. Swap the beans for **1 pound dried chickpeas**. Omit everything except the **kombu** and **salt**. Use **1 head garlic** (cloves smashed and peels removed), as well as the **zest of 1 lemon** (peeled off in long strips). Cook as written in the recipe and use anywhere you'd enjoy chickpeas.

Sage and Oregano White Beans

Use **1 pound dried cannellini, navy, lima, or gigante beans**. Swap the herbs listed for **½ bunch each of fresh sage and oregano**, tied together with kitchen twine. Toss in a **rind of Parmesan** for extra saltiness if you have one. Cook as written in the recipe. Remove the bundle of herbs and Parm rind. Serve alongside crusty bread, or use in Brothy Cavatelli and Beans (page 146).

PUT IT TO USE

Spooned over buttered rice or grilled bread

Brothy Cavatelli and Beans (page 146)

Roasted Veg over Toasted Coriander Polenta (page 134)

Component-Cooked Lunch Assemblies (page 124) and Component-Cooked Dinner Assemblies (page 150)

WHICH BEANS?

Empower yourself to step beyond canned beans, which are cooked in water without herbs or spices. You'll spend a lot of energy and ingredients trying to get a canned bean to taste like much of anything. When you cook beans from dried, your seasonings penetrate all the way into the bean as it rehydrates, making every bite deeply flavorful. Dried beans can also be purchased in bulk, which cuts down on packaging and saves you money on your grocery trips.

When it comes to varieties, the classics, like cannellini, pinto, black, and kidney, are great places to start. A benefit of opting for dried over canned is the joy of exploring. My local co-op offers lima beans and pigeon peas in bulk, and specialty food stores will often carry heirloom varieties worth discovering.

WHOLE POACHED CHICKEN

Serves 4

Cooking a whole chicken can be as simple as simmering it in a pot of water. I typically serve large pieces of bone-in meat on the first night. Whatever is left gets removed from the bone (I save the bones for scrap stock, see page 34) and shredded, which can be stirred into a big batch of chicken salad, donabe rice, or soup (use the cooking liquid as the base instead of stock).

This recipe calls for slowly bringing the water up to temperature—don't skip this. Blasting a cold chicken on high heat can cause the meat to become tough.

Gluten-free

---

1 whole chicken (2½ to 3½ pounds)

2 tablespoons sea salt

2 medium carrots, scrubbed and cut into 1-inch chunks

2 celery stalks, cut into 1-inch chunks

1 yellow or red onion (peeled if you'd like), quartered

2 dried bay leaves

Nice-to-have additions: 1 to 2 handfuls of mixed fresh (or 1 tablespoon dried) herbs, such as sage, rosemary, thyme, oregano, or tarragon

Poach the chicken: Place the chicken in a large pot and sprinkle with the salt. Arrange the vegetables, bay leaves, and any other herbs in the pot and add cold water to cover.

Place the pot over medium-low heat, partially cover the pot, and let the mixture slowly come to a bare simmer (small bubbles will form at the edges of the pot, which can take up to an hour). As foam begins to appear on the surface, use a large, flat spoon to gently skim it off.

Increase the heat to medium and continue to cook, partially covered, until the chicken is just cooked through (the internal temperature of the thickest part of the thigh should reach at least 160°F. Start checking at 30 minutes—it will take longer for larger birds. As the chicken cooks, add more water as needed to keep the chicken covered, and adjust the heat as needed to maintain a gentle simmer.

Carve the chicken and serve: Turn off the heat. Reserving the poaching liquid, remove the chicken from the pot and transfer to a cutting board placed inside a sheet pan (to catch drips). Let the chicken and the poaching liquid cool slightly, about 10 minutes.

Carve the chicken, removing the skin (save it, along with the chicken carcass, for $0 Scrap Stock, page 34).

Store the broth: Strain the reserved poaching liquid through a fine-mesh sieve into a large bowl to save as a light chicken broth, discarding the spent herbs and vegetables. Let cool to warm room temperature, about 20 minutes, then transfer to airtight containers. Poaching liquid will last in the fridge for up to 4 days or in the freezer for up to 6 months.

PUT IT TO USE

Leftover Chicken and Mushroom Donabe Rice (page 129)

Shredded Chicken Salad with Yogurt and Fennel (page 107)

Component-Cooked Assemblies: Lunch (page 124) and Dinner (page 150)

SOFT-BOILED EGGS

This method will work with however many eggs you'd like, just use a bigger or smaller pot. Bring refrigerated eggs to room temperature quickly by placing them in a bowl of hot (not boiling) water for about 5 minutes before adding to the pot of boiling water.

Gluten-free

---

5 eggs, at room temperature

Set up a large bowl of ice and water and have near the stove. Bring a medium saucepan of water to a boil over high heat. When it comes to a boil, use a spoon to gently place the eggs into the water. Reduce the heat to medium-high and let the eggs boil for 7 minutes.

Drain the water and place the eggs in the bowl of ice water to cool for at least 10 minutes.

When you're ready to eat, tap the shells all over, then peel. Store leftover eggs, unpeeled, in the refrigerator for up to 2 days.

NOTE: If you prefer hard-boiled eggs, let them cook for 11 minutes, then cool and store in the fridge for up to 1 week.

PUT IT TO USE

Bitter Greens with Black Vinegar (page 114)

Roasted Veg over Toasted Coriander Polenta (page 134)

Soothing Rice Porridge (page 95)

Component-Cooked Assemblies: Lunch (page 124) and Dinner (page 150)

EASIEST RICE

Makes about 3 cups

I married into a Japanese family, so short-grain (sometimes labeled "sushi") rice is a prerequisite for any complete meal. I also love to cook a longer-grain, American-style rice topped generously with butter and green herbs. A batch of rice can be temperamental on your first try: Using too much water makes the rice mushy, while using too little water won't let it cook through. When making Japanese rice, I use the old-school method of placing my index finger on top of the rice and adding just enough water to reach the first knuckle of my finger.

Keep in mind that different types of rice may cook differently. A rice cooker is foolproof but takes longer than a humble pot. For stovetop rice, you'll get a feel for your desired texture and the perfect amount of water to add over time.

Gluten-free, vegan

---

1 cup short-grain white rice

Water or preferred stock (see $0 Scrap Stock, page 34)

Pinch of sea salt (optional)

NOTE: To keep uncooked rice fresh for longer, store in airtight containers rather than the bag it came in.

Wash the rice (see opposite page). Leave to soak for 30 minutes (or up to 3 hours) before cooking for the bounciest texture.

Stovetop Method

Transfer the washed rice to a medium pot or donabe and add 1¼ cups water and salt (if using). Cover the pot and let the mixture come to a simmer over medium-low heat, about 15 minutes (you should hear a faint crackling sound). Turn off the heat and allow the rice to steam for another 15 minutes. Don't take the lid off to check on it. Uncover and use a wooden spoon or rice paddle to fluff up the rice. The water should be completely absorbed and rice should be cooked through at this point; if not, re-cover and steam for another 5 to 10 minutes.

Rice Cooker Method

Transfer the washed rice to the pot of the rice cooker. Add water according to the corresponding fill line. Cook the rice following the instructions on your rice cooker. When the rice is cooked, use a wooden spoon or rice paddle to fluff the rice, return the lid for 10 minutes to steam, then serve.

Best eaten immediately: I always make rice fresh instead of storing and rewarming it. A rice cooker's "keep warm" setting makes it easy to make the rice in advance and serve when you're ready.

PUT IT TO USE

HOW TO WASH RICE

Always wash rice before cooking. Rinsing the rice removes excess starch from the grains that can create a gummy, overly sticky final texture, as opposed to fluffy cooked grains. Measure out the rice into a glass bowl, top it with water, gently swish around the mixture with your fingers, and then pour the water off into the sink, making sure not to pour the rice grains with it. Repeat until the water runs relatively clear, usually about 3 rinses.

Variations: Butter Rice, Two Ways

Shoyu Butter Rice

Cook Easiest Rice as written. Spoon rice into serving bowls. Use your finger (or the handle of a wooden spoon) to make a divot in the center of each bowl of rice. Place a **big pat of butter** in the divot, then drizzle with your best **soy sauce**.

Garlic and Parsley Butter Rice

Instead of short-grain rice, use **Carolina Gold** or another long-grain white rice and **1¾ cups water**. To the washed rice, add **2 cloves of finely chopped garlic**. Cook as written in Easiest Rice. Before fluffing the rice, add **¼ cup finely chopped parsley** and **1 tablespoon unsalted butter**. As you fluff the rice, you'll mix in the parsley and encourage the butter to melt. Season with more **salt** to taste.

COOKING WITH A DONABE

Donabe (pronounced doh-nah-beh) translates to "clay pot" in Japanese. You'll see a donabe used throughout the Japanese-style recipes in this book. It's excellent for steaming and slow-cooking over the stovetop. I like to use ours for rice dishes and stews. If you don't have one, a heavy-bottomed pot will suffice for most recipes.

BROTH-SIMMERED FARRO

Makes about 3 cups

Nutty, chewy farro is one of my favorite nutritious grains to keep in rotation for lunch and dinner. Often, farro is sold as pearled or semi-pearled, which is the process of removing all or part of the outer bran. I prefer whole farro, which takes a little longer to cook but has a firmer texture. You can tell which farro you have by checking the label on your package. Any variety works for this recipe.

Vegan option

---

1 cup farro, preferably whole/unpearled (see Note)

2 cups preferred stock (see $0 Scrap Stock, page 34), plus more as needed

1 medium carrot or 2 celery stalks, finely chopped

Nice-to-have additions: 1 dried bay leaf, ½ teaspoon freshly ground black pepper, 1 teaspoon ground coriander (or 2 teaspoons crushed coriander seeds), 3 smashed and peeled garlic cloves

Sea salt

Add the dried or presoaked farro to a fine-mesh sieve and rinse off with water. In a medium pot, combine the farro and stock. Stir in the carrot and any nice-to-have additions if using.

Bring the mixture to a gentle boil over medium heat. Reduce the heat to medium-low and simmer, stirring occasionally, until the farro is just tender (start checking at 15 minutes, but whole farro may take up to 40). Add more stock if needed if it's absorbed before the farro is done cooking. Drain the farro in a sieve. Spread the farro onto a sheet pan (this will help it cool quickly) and season with salt to taste. Let sit until it's room temperature, about 15 minutes.

Store cooked farro in an airtight container in the refrigerator for up to 4 days.

NOTE: To speed up the cooking time of whole farro, soak it: Place the rinsed farro in a bowl covered with a couple inches of water and refrigerate for at least 6 hours, or overnight. When cooking soaked farro, start testing for doneness at about 15 minutes.

PUT IT TO USE

Crispy-Skinned Salmon over Herbed Farro (page 149)

"Instant" Any-Veg Soup (page 133)

Component-Cooked Assemblies: Lunch (page 124) and Dinner (page 150)

BRINE-BOILED VEG

This is the easiest way to get a large amount of produce prepped for the week ahead. Brine-boiled potatoes can be quickly fried up to accompany eggs for breakfast (see Crispy Breakfast Potatoes, page 92) and brine-boiled cauliflower is delicious stirred into Curried Lentil Stew (page 132). I love green beans cooked this way straight out of the pot as a snack—but they're also great coated with a quick sesame sauce (see Green Bean Gomae, page 103).

Gluten-free, vegan

Bring a **large pot of water** to a boil over medium-high heat. Salt generously, even more than pasta water (about **⅓ cup sea salt** per 6 quarts water). Drop **1 pound vegetables** into the boiling water and cook until the color deepens or brightens and the pieces are just fork-tender (see the opposite page for specifics).

Once you've got a pot of salty water going, cook a few different kinds of veg back-to-back, removing each batch with tongs to a colander. If you're boiling something starchy, like potatoes, or strongly flavored, like asparagus, save those for last. Store drained brine-boiled veg in airtight containers in the refrigerator for up to 1 week.

PUT IT TO USE

Crispy Breakfast Potatoes (page 92)

Curried Lentil Stew (page 132)

"Instant" Any-Veg Soup (page 133)

Component-Cooked Assemblies: Lunch (page 124) and Dinner (page 150)

Asparagus

Rinse and snap off the woody bottom portion of the spears. Cook until bright green and tender, 2 to 5 minutes (the thinner the spears, the faster they'll cook).

Broccoli and Cauliflower

Slice long stems off the crown and trim off the tough outer peel. Chop the stem into ½-inch chunks. Split the crown into 1-inch florets. Cook until just tender, 3 minutes, or up to 6 minutes for a softer texture.

Carrots and Parsnips

Scrub and peel if desired, then slice into ½-inch chunks. Cook until fork-tender, 3 to 6 minutes.

Green Beans

I like skinny haricots verts, but check your farmers' market for varieties like Romano, wax, and long beans. Cook until just tender, about 2 minutes for haricots verts, or up to 4 to 6 minutes for thicker beans.

Leafy Greens

Wash a bunch of kale, Swiss chard, or collard greens, then slice into 2-inch ribbons. (You can strip the leaves from the stem and midrib if you prefer, but I like the stem's extra crunch.) Cook until the leaves turn dark green, 30 seconds (hardy greens will take longer). I like to pour over a splash of apple cider vinegar while these are still cooling in the colander.

Potatoes

Scrub waxy potatoes such as yellow, red, fingerling, new, or baby potatoes (no need to peel); or scrub and peel starchy potatoes, such as Russet, and cut as needed into 1- or 2-inch chunks. It's best not to mix varieties, which can have different cooking times, but if everything is about the same size they'll be okay. Cook until a paring knife easily slides in—start checking at 10 minutes.

Turnips and Beets

Scrub and peel, trim any greens (save for Greens for Breakfast, page 80), and cut into 1-inch chunks. Cook until a paring knife easily slides in—start checking at 10 minutes.

Winter Squash (such as Butternut, Acorn, Kabocha)

Scrub and peel the squash, then slice into ½-inch chunks. Cook until fork-tender, about 5 minutes.

Zucchini and Summer Squash

Slice the squash into ½-inch chunks. Cook until just tender, 2 to 3 minutes.

MIX-AND-SIT PICKLES

These pickles are fermented, which means they're full of naturally occurring probiotics. Just like kimchi and sauerkraut, this method works by mixing vegetables with a precise amount of salt and then leaving them to ferment. I always keep at least one of these pickles on hand in my fridge—they're the perfect healthy snack or side for a meal. Get started by trying one of the recipes below, or explore on your own with my Lacto-Fermenting Formula (see opposite page).

YOU'LL NEED:

A kitchen scale
Sea salt (not iodized table salt)
Glass jars (thoroughly cleaned)
Large glass mixing bowl
Your favorite vegetables
Fermentation weights (or small zip-top bags)

Fermentation-Friendly Veg

This technique works great for nearly any sturdy raw vegetables, like cucumbers, carrots, cabbage, fennel, turnips, radishes, green beans, beets, and peppers.

For extra flavor and nutrients, you can also add peeled raw ginger or turmeric root, onions, garlic, peppercorns, and whole aromatic seeds like mustard, dill, caraway, and fennel.

No Vinegar?

If we're being literal, *pickling* refers to curing foods in vinegar. The resulting pickles are also delicious but not fermented or probiotic. For truly "pickled" pickles, see Sweet and Zingy Quick Pickles (page 58).

PUT IT TO USE

Anywhere you'd enjoy an extra zingy crunch, from rice bowls to alongside roast chicken.

THE LACTO-FERMENTING FORMULA

GRAB JARS

One-quart mason jars are large enough to fit a good amount of produce, but you can use any size you have on hand. Make sure the jars you use are thoroughly cleaned.

PREP PRODUCE

Peel and chop your veg into uniform pieces that will fit in the jar.

WEIGH IT OUT

Place the jar on a kitchen scale set to grams and zero-out the weight. Fill tightly with the chopped veg and any other seasonings (like seeds or herbs). Pour in enough filtered water* to cover the veg, leaving about 1 inch of space from the top of the jar. Write down the weight displayed on the scale.

CALCULATE SALT

Multiply the weight of the veg and water by 2.5%—that's how many grams of salt you'll need to add. For example, 100 grams of ingredients would be 100 × 0.025 = 2.5 grams (or ½ teaspoon) of sea salt.

TOP IT OFF

Sprinkle in the salt. Make sure to submerge any floating bits of veg below the surface of the brine to prevent exposing them to oxygen. You can buy fermentation weights to stack on top of the veg, or just use a small zip-top bag filled with water. Screw the lid onto the jar.

LET IT SIT

Set the jar inside a shallow bowl or on a sheet pan (as the vegetables ferment, the liquid can start to seep out). Transfer to a cool, dark place and leave to sit for 24 hours. After 24 hours, unscrew the lid, without opening it all the way, to "burp" it, which releases the pressure that builds as the mixture starts to ferment. Continue to burp daily, until the fizzing subsides and the liquid is a little cloudy. (If your ferment smells foul or develops spots of black or blue mold, toss and start over.)

TASTE!

Your pickles are ready when they taste salty-tangy and have softened slightly. The exact timing will depend on the temperature of the room. They may be ready after only 5 days, or if it's cooler, you may need to go up to 14 days. Store in the same jar in the refrigerator for up to 3 months.

*If using watery produce like cabbage, you won't add extra water (see Purple Cabbage Curtido, page 57), letting the salt draw out the vegetable's natural moisture.

GINGERED CARROTS

Makes about 2 quarts

These crunchy, probiotic carrots are my family's favorite out-of-the-fridge snack.

Gluten-free, vegan

2 teaspoons caraway seeds

2 teaspoons black peppercorns

2 small onions (4oz each), red, yellow, or white, sliced ¼ inch thick (120g)

½ cup (85g) thinly sliced peeled fresh ginger

5 large carrots (14oz total), scrubbed, halved lengthwise, sliced into ½-inch-thick spears (500g)

4 cups (960g) filtered water

2 tablespoons plus 2 teaspoons sea salt

Wash one 2-quart or two 1-quart mason jars. Place the caraway and peppercorns in the bottom of the jar(s), then layer over the onions and ginger. (I add these first as they're lighter in weight and tend to float.) Pack in the carrots on top. Pour in the water and sprinkle with the salt.

Weight down the vegetables (see page 53). Screw the lid on the jar(s). Set the jar(s) inside a shallow bowl or on a sheet pan and transfer to a cool, dark place, like a kitchen cabinet or closet. Let sit for 24 hours.

Unseal the jar(s) without opening all the way (this is known as "burping"). Re-cover with the lid(s) and continue to ferment, burping the jar(s) daily, until the fizzing subsides and the liquid is starting to look a bit cloudy. The exact timing depends on the temperature of your room: If it's warm inside, start checking them after 5 days; if it's cooler, you may need to go up to 14 days. Taste a carrot: It should taste lightly briny and earthy, and be crunchy in texture. Screw on the lid(s) and transfer the jar(s) to the refrigerator. Eat within 3 months.

PUT IT TO USE

House Niçoise (page 116)

Soothing Rice Porridge (page 95)

Component-Cooked Assemblies: Lunch (page 124) and Dinner (page 150)

CLASSIC DILL PICKLES

Makes about 2 quarts

Any cucumber will ferment well, but for the classic experience, look for Kirby or other pickling varieties, plentiful at farmers' markets in late summer.

Glunte-free, vegan option

2 teaspoons coriander seeds

1 teaspoon caraway seeds

1 teaspoon black peppercorns

2 dried or fresh bay leaves

6 large garlic cloves (30g), peeled

¼ cup (3g) fresh dill sprigs

10 small pickling cucumbers (500g total), such as Kirby, washed

4 cups (960g) filtered water

2 tablespoons plus 1½ teaspoons sea salt

Wash one 2-quart or two 1-quart mason jars. Place the coriander seeds, caraway, peppercorns, and bay leaves in the bottom of the jar(s), then add the garlic and dill.

Trim the blossom end of each cucumber and pack in the cucumbers. (Leave the cucumbers whole, but you can halve or quarter the last one to squeeze everything in.)

Pour in the water and sprinkle in the salt.

Weight down the vegetables (see page 53). Screw the lid on the jar(s). Set the jar(s) inside a shallow bowl or on a sheet pan and transfer to a cool, dark place, like a kitchen cabinet or closet. Let sit for 24 hours.

Unseal the jar(s) without opening all the way (this is known as "burping"). Re-cover with the lid(s) and continue to ferment, burping the jar(s) daily, until the fizzing subsides and the liquid is starting to look a bit cloudy. The exact timing depends on the temperature of your room; if it's warm inside, start checking them after 5 days, or if it's cooler, you may need to go up to 14 days. Taste a pickle: It should taste like your favorite packaged dill pickles (!) and be crunchy in texture. Screw on the lid(s) and transfer the jar(s) to the refrigerator. Eat within 3 months.

PUT IT TO USE

Component-Cooked Assemblies: Lunch (page 124) and Dinner (page 150)

PURPLE CABBAGE CURTIDO

Makes about 2 quarts

Curtido is an herby cabbage slaw that originates in El Salvador. My version uses red cabbage for a brilliantly vibrant color. Use it anywhere you'd reach for sauerkraut. Because cabbage contains a lot of water, I like to use a dry-salting technique, which involves vigorously massaging the cabbage with salt to break the cell walls and let out excess water, which creates the brine.

Gluten-free, vegan

---

1 large head red cabbage (about 2 pounds), 2 leaves reserved whole, the rest very thinly sliced (900g)

2 tablespoons sea salt

1 large carrot (3½ ounces), scrubbed

1 medium red onion (6 ounces), thinly sliced (150g)

1 jalapeño (15g), stemmed and thinly sliced (optional)

2 tablespoons coriander seeds

1 tablespoon caraway seeds

2 teaspoons dried oregano

Add the cabbage and salt to a large bowl. Use your clean hands to scrunch and massage the cabbage mixture for 2 to 3 minutes, until it is softened and has begun to release water.

Use a vegetable peeler to slice the carrot into ribbons (you should have about 100g). Add to the bowl with the cabbage, along with the onion, jalapeño (if using), seeds, and oregano. Toss well with your hands to combine, scrunching more to soften the vegetables as you go.

Cover the bowl with a kitchen towel or cheesecloth and let it sit for 1 hour. Use clean hands to massage the mixture again until the vegetables have released even more water and the cabbage is deeply purple and very soft.

Wash one 2-quart or two 1-quart mason jars. Pack the cabbage mixture into the jar(s). Pour any excess liquid from the bowl into the jar(s), leaving at least 1 inch of headspace. The vegetables should be covered with liquid—if not, add filtered water until it does. Press a reserved whole cabbage leaf into the jar(s), further packing down the vegetables; this will act as your fermentation weight.

Screw on the lid(s), placing the jar(s) on a plate to avoid any bubbling over and store in a dark, cool location. Let sit for 24 hours.

Unseal the jar(s) without opening all the way (this is known as "burping"). Cover with the lid(s) and continue to ferment, burping the jar(s) daily, for 1 week. The curtido will smell similar to sauerkraut and taste pleasantly sour and a bit crunchy. Transfer the jar(s) to the refrigerator and eat within 3 months.

PUT IT TO USE

House Niçoise (page 116)

Component-Cooked Assemblies: Lunch (page 124) and Dinner (page 150)

SWEET AND ZINGY QUICK PICKLES

Makes about 1 quart

These are pickles you don't have to wait for. Any vegetable that you would use in Mix-and-Sit Pickles (page 52) works here, but you'll be using a hot vinegar brine instead of fermenting anything.

Gluten-free, vegan

- 1 pound crunchy vegetables, such as carrots, Japanese turnips, fennel, radish, cucumber, and/or cauliflower
- 2 teaspoons black peppercorns
- 2 teaspoons coriander seeds
- 1 teaspoon fennel seeds
- 1 cup filtered water
- ½ cup distilled white vinegar
- ½ cup apple cider vinegar or red wine vinegar
- 2 dried bay leaves
- 1 tablespoon cane sugar
- 1 teaspoon sea salt

Wash the veg and slice into roughly 1-inch pieces. Pack the veg tightly into a clean 1-quart or two 1-pint glass mason jars.

In a medium saucepan, toast the peppercorns, coriander, and fennel seeds over medium-high heat, swirling the pan often, until fragrant, about 45 seconds. Stir in the water, both vinegars, the bay leaves, sugar, and salt. Bring to a gentle boil, then reduce the heat to medium and let simmer for 5 minutes.

Turn off the heat and allow the brine to sit for another 5 minutes to cool slightly. Pour the brine into the jar(s)—it should just cover the veg. Let the mixture cool to room temperature, about 15 minutes.

Screw on the lid(s) and transfer the jar(s) to the fridge. The pickles are best after sitting for at least 24 hours, and will stay fresh in the refrigerator for up to 2 months.

Variation

Quick-Pickled Ginger

If you want to make quick-pickled ginger, wash, peel, and thinly slice **1 pound of ginger root**. Swap the apple cider vinegar for **unseasoned rice vinegar** and add an extra tablespoon of **sugar**.

PUT IT TO USE

House Niçoise (page 116)

Component-Cooking Assemblies: Lunch (page 124) and Dinner (page 150)

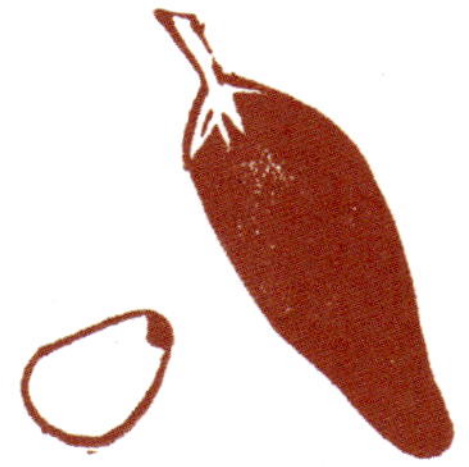

QUICK-FERMENTED GREEN HOT SAUCE

Makes about 2 cups

This recipe can replace any vinegar-based hot sauce that you're used to buying off the shelf. It's lightly fermented over a couple of days, but you can also use it right away if you don't want to wait. Swap out the green chiles and green bell pepper for red chiles and red bell pepper if you prefer a red version.

Gluten-free

---

8 ounces fresh green chiles (6 to 8 large), such as jalapeño or serrano

4 ounces green bell pepper (1 large), cut into 2-inch chunks (157g)

1 tablespoon sea salt

1¼ cups (288g) apple cider vinegar

2 teaspoons honey

NOTE: If your skin is sensitive, wear gloves when stemming and slicing the chiles.

If you'd like the hot sauce on the milder side, remove the seeds and ribs from half or all of the chiles, then cut into 2-inch chunks (you should have about 200 grams).

In a food processor or blender, combine the chiles, bell pepper, and salt. Pulse until a coarse puree forms. Pour the mixture into a clean 1-quart jar (it will not be totally full). Seal the jar and let it sit at room temperature for 12 hours, until the mixture gets a bit juicier.

Open the jar and stir in the vinegar and honey. Reseal the jar and let sit at room temperature for another 12 hours or up to 1 week (burp the jar daily to release pressure). The finished hot sauce will not be totally smooth. Transfer the hot sauce to the refrigerator and use within 3 months.

BAKED WHOLE SWEET POTATOES

At the start of every week, I bake a few sweet potatoes (orange or a Japanese variety, which have white flesh and are starchier) whole until the kitchen smells of caramelized sugar. A sweet potato is the perfect quick addition to round out a weekday lunch, but I also love it as a sweet treat—drizzle with tahini, cinnamon, maple syrup, and a pinch of salt. Yum.

Gluten-free, vegan

4 medium sweet potatoes (about 6 ounces each), scrubbed

Preheat the oven to 425°F. Line the bottom of a heavy-bottomed pot, such as a Dutch oven, with parchment paper.

Place the sweet potatoes in the pot. Cover the pot and bake until completely tender when poked with a fork and starting to caramelize (you'll see a bit of brown sugary liquid forming on the bottom of the pot), about 1½ hours (the larger the potato, the longer the cook time).

Let cool slightly and serve. Or cool to room temperature and store in an airtight container in the refrigerator for up to 1 week.

NOTE: Select sweet potatoes that are all about the same size for an even cook time. Be sure to scrub the skins well, and then actually eat them. (A lot of the best nutrients are loaded in the skins of your produce.)

PUT IT TO USE

Japanese Sweet Potato Loaf (page 193)

Component-Cooked Assemblies: Lunch (page 124) and Dinner (page 150)

THE PERFECT SHEET PAN VEG

A standard half-sheet pan is my favorite tool for making vegetables with a fork-tender inside and a delightfully caramelized exterior. In the same way that you'd preheat a skillet on the stovetop, adding your vegetables to an already-hot pan helps to develop a nice golden sear without overcooking.

Gluten-free, vegan

Place **about 2 pounds of veg** in a large bowl and toss with a **few pinches of sea salt, some black pepper,** and a **glug of extra-virgin olive oil** (the exact amount of oil isn't important; the veg should be well-coated in oil but not swimming).

Preheat the oven to 425°F with a sheet pan inside—by the time the oven is preheated, so is your pan.

Remove the hot sheet pan from the oven and quickly add the veg in a single layer, with one cut-side down. If you run out of space on the pan, don't crowd it—just hold the extras aside for another round of roasting. You should hear a sizzle when the veg hits the pan.

Return the sheet pan to the oven. Roast, tossing after 15 minutes, and continuing to cook until the veg is fork-tender, another 10 to 20 minutes depending on the veg, and golden brown.

Store cooled veg in an airtight container in the refrigerator for up to 4 days.

NOTE: It's best to bake each vegetable separately to accommodate unique cook times (for example, fennel or zucchini will cook more quickly than winter squash). Alternatively, to cook several varieties of vegetable at once, toss each in oil separately and spread out in separate areas on the sheet pan, removing each from the pan when they become tender.

The Perfect Sheet Pan Vegetables and How to Slice Them

Fennel

Trim any fronds and stalks from the bulbs (save for $0 Scrap Stock, page 34), then slice into 1-inch-thick wedges.

Carrots

Scrub and halve (or quarter if more than 2 inches thick) lengthwise.

Winter squash

Halve, scoop out the seeds, then peel (especially for thick-skinned butternut and acorn squash) and cut into 2-inch pieces.

Summer squash and zucchini

Skin on, cut into ½-inch-thick rounds.

Broccoli, cauliflower, and cabbage

Peel the fibrous skin from the stems of broccoli stalks or trim the core of a cabbage, then slice the heads into quarters.

Fingerling and baby potatoes

Scrub and halve.

Larger potatoes (including sweet potatoes)

Scrub and cut into ½-inch-thick pieces.

PUT IT TO USE

Roasted Veg over Toasted Coriander Polenta (page 134)
Weeknight Roast Chicken Dinner (page 138)
Component-Cooked Assemblies: Lunch (page 124) and Dinner (page 150)

1-2-3 SAUCE

Each recipe makes about 1¼ cups

Quick sauces are a beautifully easy way to make simply cooked food (roast vegetables, poached chicken) truly exciting to eat. These two all-purpose sauces, made with tahini or yogurt, have a ratio that's easy to remember (1, 2, 3) and work with staples you likely already have on hand.

1-2-3 TAHINI SAUCE

In a medium bowl, whisk together **1 cup tahini, 2 tablespoons soy sauce,** and **3 tablespoons water** until smooth. Season to taste with **salt and pepper.**

Store in an airtight container in the refrigerator for up to 3 days.

1-2-3 YOGURT SAUCE

In a medium bowl, whisk together **1 cup whole milk Greek yogurt, 2 finely chopped garlic cloves,** and **3 tablespoons fresh lemon juice.** Season to taste with **salt and pepper.**

Store in an airtight container in the refrigerator for up to 3 days.

PUT IT TO USE

Golden Veggie Pancakes (page 119)

Sweet Potato and Lamb Meatballs (page 142)

Component-Cooked Assemblies: Lunch (page 124) and Dinner (page 150)

NUTS 'N' HERBS SAUCE

Makes about 1 cup

A bright, easy, clean-out-the-fridge sauce for everyday use.

Gluten-free, vegan

Grate the zest of **1 lemon** into a blender or food processor. Halve the lemon and squeeze in the juice. Add **3 coarsely chopped scallions, 2 tightly packed cups of coarsely chopped tender herbs, ⅓ cup extra-virgin olive oil, ¼ cup toasted nuts,** and **3 tablespoons water.** Season with a **generous pinch of salt** and a **few grinds of pepper.** Blend until smooth, adding more water by the tablespoon as needed. Season with more salt and pepper to taste.

Store in an airtight container in the refrigerator for up to 3 days.

PUT IT TO USE

Golden Veggie Pancakes (page 119)

Roasted Veg over Toasted Coriander Polenta (page 134)

Weeknight Roast Chicken Dinner (page 138)

Component-Cooked Assemblies: Lunch (page 124) and Dinner (page 150)

ANY TOASTED NUT OR SEED

I like adding nuts and seeds to at least one meal every day. Toasting them enhances their crunchy texture and brings out a deeper, aromatic flavor. Store them in the refrigerator and sprinkle liberally on breakfast, lunch, or dinner.

Gluten-free, vegan

Preheat the oven to 325°F.

Spread **nuts or seeds** (any amount that fits in a single layer) on a sheet pan and bake, checking for doneness and stirring every 5 minutes, until the nuts smell toasty and have darkened slightly in color. Depending on the nut or seed, this can take 6 to 15 minutes.

Let cool completely, then store in an airtight container in the refrigerator.

YOUR OWN BREAD CRUMBS

Bread crumbs can be made easily from any leftover stale bread—one less thing to buy, and a great way to use what you would otherwise throw away.

Gluten-free, vegan (depending on bread used)

When you have **leftover stale crusty bread**, such as sourdough boule or a baguette, cut it into chunks and let it dry out completely in a paper bag (a couple days is great). Add those chunks to a blender or food processor and blend until they reach a sandy consistency.

Store fresh bread crumbs in an airtight container in the refrigerator.

SKILLET JAM

Makes about 2 cups

Jam is beyond easy to make at home. My recipe is stored in the fridge instead of canned for a long shelf life. This way you can use much less sugar and don't need to worry about precision in the recipe ratios or a complex preservation technique. It's an especially great use for fruit that's gone a little soft. (The recipe is easily multiplied for whatever quantity of fruit you have.) Any berries or stone fruit like peaches, plums, and cherries will work well here. In the wintertime, I use mixed frozen berries with beautiful results. It's cooked hot and fast: Don't be afraid to turn up your burner, but keep stirring as it thickens to prevent the sugars from burning.

Gluten-free, vegan

⅔ cup cane sugar

2 to 3 tablespoons grated lemon, grapefruit, or orange zest

6 cups fresh or frozen berries, or chopped very ripe stone fruit

¼ cup fresh lemon, grapefruit, or orange juice

½ teaspoon sea salt

In a stainless steel or cast-iron skillet, combine the sugar and citrus zest. Rub the zest into the sugar with your fingers until it's slightly moistened and fragrant. Stir in the fruit, citrus juice, and salt.

Place the skillet over high heat and cook the mixture, stirring occasionally, until the juices come to a simmer, about 5 minutes. Continue to cook, stirring often and mashing the fruit with the back of a spoon until it's thick enough that you can drag the spoon across the pot and no liquid immediately rushes in to fill the bare spot, 10 to 15 minutes.

Turn off the heat and continue stirring for another minute or so to encourage the jam to cool a bit. You can eat it warm now, or transfer to a heatproof jar or container and let cool to warm room temperature. Cover and store in the refrigerator for up to 1 week.

PUT IT TO USE

Celebration Cake (page 215)

Lemon Berry Syrup (page 157)

GOOD

MORNINGS

I resisted adding a breakfast chapter to this book because I believe that weekday mornings belong to the un-recipe. I like my morning meals to be simple, repeatable, and comforting—this is not the moment for a cooking project. These recipes are uncomplicated, and several require no cooking at all. The objective is simple: Get to the table.

Our weekday breakfasts are straightforward, but they still leave a little room for genuine enjoyment. In the face of a protein bar, a bowl of yogurt drizzled with good olive oil and salt is absolutely revelatory. Great ingredients, easily assembled, make a moment worth pausing for.

Breakfast was about the best part of the day. There was an almost mysterious feeling about passing through the night and awakening to a new day. Everyone greeted each other in the morning with gladness and a real sense of gratefulness to see the new day.

—*Edna Lewis,* The Taste of Country Cooking

MATCHA 101

Matcha is a powdered Japanese green tea that's been enjoyed in Japan for centuries. Because you consume the entire tea leaf, matcha has considerably higher amounts of chlorophyll and amino acids than a cup of steeped green tea. Thanks to the calming amino acid L-theanine, matcha provides a smoother energy than coffee, with fewer jitters and no crash.

With surging interest in matcha green tea, there's a lot of talk about how to find "the good stuff." Most companies (mine included) will label their higher-quality matcha as "ceremonial grade," which means that the tea would be appropriate for a traditional tea ceremony. If a matcha product is listed as "culinary grade," the flavor may be too bitter and bold to enjoy outside of baked goods or generously sweetened lattes. There is no formal differentiation between ceremonial and culinary grade matcha, so it's best to look for the following indicators of quality: bright green color, shade-grown and stone-ground tea leaves, cultivated in Japan.

Matcha production in Japan is not limited to only one prefecture, but Uji, in Kyoto, is the original home of matcha. Many of the best matcha powders are produced there, including the one we source for Golde.

Ultimately, matcha is a natural product that will have variations in flavor based on the region and even the weather conditions of a particular year. The best way to find a matcha you love is to explore and taste from a source you trust.

To make a traditional matcha, you'll need a bamboo whisk (*chasen*) and a ceramic matcha bowl (*chawan*). At Golde, we also offer an electric whisk, which is nice for convenience. Don't try to use a metal cooking whisk for this—you'll end up with a clumpy drink that isn't well combined.

MORNING MATCHA

Each recipe serves 1

We started Golde with a turmeric blend in 2017 and eventually became best known for our matcha powder. Matcha is my choice of caffeine on weekdays, because it offers serene focus in place of coffee jitters. I start by making a shot (below), which can then be used for any style of matcha drink (recipes follow).

MATCHA SHOT

Gluten-free, vegan

1 teaspoon matcha powder
1 ounce warm water

A matcha shot forms the base of a latte or other matcha-based drinks. Add a prepared matcha shot to one of the recipes on the following pages to enjoy.

Scoop the matcha powder into a matcha bowl.

Top with the warm, but not boiling, water. Boiling hot water will burn the matcha and make it taste bitter.

Use a bamboo whisk to whisk in a quick, zigzag formation until frothiness forms on top, 10 to 20 seconds.

NOTE: If you're using an electric whisk, use a high-walled vessel (like a tall glass), not a matcha bowl, to prevent spilling.

CONTINUED

Pure

CLASSIC MATCHA LATTE

Gluten-free, vegan

5 ounces (scant ⅔ cup) preferred milk

1 teaspoon maple syrup (see Note), plus more to taste

Pinch of sea salt (optional)

Matcha Shot (page 74)

For a Hot Latte

In a small pot (or microwave-safe bowl), stir together the milk, maple syrup, and salt (if using). Heat over medium-low heat until the mixture is steaming, about 5 minutes (or microwave on medium power for 15 to 30 seconds). Pour the warm milk into a mug and top with the matcha shot.

For an Iced Latte

In a small bowl, stir together the milk, maple syrup, and salt (if using). Fill a tall glass with ice. Pour the sweetened milk over the ice, then top with the matcha shot.

NOTE: I like to use maple syrup to sweeten matcha rather than honey or sugar. It's low glycemic and dissolves easily in hot or cold liquid.

MATCHA SUNRISE

Ice

5 ounces (scant ⅔ cup) freshly squeezed orange juice (from about 2 oranges)

Matcha Shot (page 74)

Fill a tall glass with ice. Pour the orange juice over the ice, then top with the matcha shot.

MATCHA AMERICANO

Matcha Shot (page 74)

5 ounces (scant ⅔ cup) hot water, cold water, or seltzer (or tonic water)

Ice (optional)

Lemon wedge (optional)

For a hot drink, add the shot and the hot water. For an iced drink, pour over the ice and top with the cold water. For a fizzy drink, combine the shot and seltzer or tonic water. A squeeze of lemon is a nice addition.

TAHINI MATCHA

5 ounces (scant ⅔ cup) hot water

2 tablespoons tahini

1 teaspoon maple syrup

Pinch of sea salt

Matcha Shot (page 74)

In a bowl, whisk together the hot water, tahini, maple syrup, and salt until smooth. Pour the warm "tahini milk" into a mug and top with the matcha shot.

A GOLDEN LATTE

Serves 1

I fell in love with turmeric as a superfood when I learned about its myriad health benefits. It's been used for centuries in Ayurveda and Traditional Chinese Medicine, and it also makes a beautifully soothing latte. This caffeine-free recipe is a golden way to start the morning.

Gluten-free, vegan

½ teaspoon ground turmeric

½ teaspoon ground cinnamon

½ teaspoon ground ginger

5 ounces (scant ⅔ cup) milk of choice

1 teaspoon maple syrup

In a small saucepan, whisk together the spices, milk, and maple syrup until smooth. Heat over medium-low until steaming and warmed through, about 5 minutes. Serve warm.

Variation

A Golden Hot Cocoa

Add **1 tablespoon cacao powder** and an additional **½ teaspoon maple syrup** along with the spices.

ON OTHER SUPERFOOD POWDERS

In addition to matcha, I always keep turmeric and cacao powder on hand. We source these ingredients to make our superfood latte blends at Golde, and I also love to use them in my cooking. Cacao, matcha, and turmeric powders can be added to smoothies, oats, and baked goods to provide unique flavor, vibrant color, and wellness benefits. Just be mindful of baking with matcha, because it will make your finished product a little caffeinated.

SOFT DASHI SCRAMBLED EGGS OVER RICE

Serves 2

These are softly scrambled eggs, perked up with umami-rich dashi and fresh scallions, that cook up in just a couple of minutes. And yes, you can use a carbon steel or stainless steel pan to scramble eggs without sticking—no need for a nonstick pan. Shiro dashi is a Japanese condiment or soup base of concentrated fish stock with other sweet, salty, and umami-rich ingredients like soy sauce and sugar. If you can't find it, see below for a quick alternative.

3 eggs

1½ teaspoons shiro dashi, or see "In Place of Shiro Dashi"

1 tablespoon extra-virgin olive oil

1 cup cooked Easiest Rice (page 44), for serving

2 scallions, thinly sliced

Toasted sesame seeds, for sprinkling

In a medium bowl, whisk together the eggs and dashi until very smooth.

Heat a medium carbon steel or stainless steel pan over medium-high heat for 1 minute.

Reduce the heat to medium, add the oil to the pan, and tilt to coat. Pour the eggs into the pan. Immediately use a fork or spatula to drag the edges of the eggs into the center as they set, tilting the pan to the side to allow the uncooked egg to run to the edges and cook. Continue dragging and tilting until the eggs are just barely cooked, about 30 seconds. The surface should still be a little shiny, but not totally wet and jiggly, and as you tilt the pan the eggs should no longer run. (If you prefer fully cooked eggs, continue cooking until the surface is matte, another 30 seconds or so.)

Flip the eggs out onto a bowl of rice, wet side up. Top with scallions and sesame seeds.

In Place of Shiro Dashi

If I don't have shiro dashi on hand, this combination yields a similar flavor profile to use in its place. You can use this as a 1:1 swap for the amount of dashi that's called for in a recipe. In a medium bowl, whisk together **⅓ cup soy sauce**, **⅓ cup cane sugar**, and **2 tablespoons fish sauce** until smooth. Store in an airtight container in the refrigerator. Makes about ¾ cup.

GREENS FOR BREAKFAST

Serves 2

Hardy greens, cooked in garlic and well salted, make the perfect pairing for your morning eggs. This is my favorite technique for making them because it keeps the texture a little crispy and the flavors bright.

Gluten-free, vegan

---

2 tablespoons extra-virgin olive oil

½ pound hardy greens, such as kale, Swiss chard, or broccoli rabe, midribs removed, leaves thinly sliced

2 garlic cloves, thinly sliced

2 teaspoons fresh lemon juice

Flaky sea salt and freshly ground black pepper

In a large skillet, heat the oil over medium-high heat until it ripples. Add the greens in a single layer. Cover with a lid (or a sheet pan) and increase the heat to high. Cook until the greens are wilted and just starting to char, about 5 minutes.

Uncover and flip the greens with tongs. Sprinkle in the garlic, cover, and cook until the greens are totally wilted, another 5 minutes.

Turn off the heat and uncover. Drizzle in the lemon juice and sprinkle with salt and pepper. Toss and season with salt and pepper to taste before serving.

SERVE WITH

Issey's Buttery Omelet (page 91)

Soft Dashi Scrambled Eggs over Rice (page 79)

Soft-Boiled Eggs (page 43)

5 january 2025

SIMPLE STEEL-CUT OATMEAL

Serves 2

When it comes to oats, I always choose steel-cut for a chewy, hearty texture that's also more filling. They take a bit longer to cook than rolled oats, but I find the 30 minutes that they're on the stovetop to be a nice opportunity for pause in the morning. Keep it interesting by adding chopped dried fruit, nuts, warming spices, or even a spoonful of freshly made Skillet Jam (page 68).

Gluten-free (use GF oats), vegan option

---

2 cups water, plus more as needed

½ cup steel-cut oats

Pinch of sea salt

Whole milk (optional), for serving

Salted or unsalted butter (optional), for serving

Raw honey (optional), for serving

In a small saucepan, bring the water to a boil over medium-high heat. Stir in the oats and salt, reduce the heat to medium-low, and cook, stirring often, until the mixture has thickened and the grains are tender, 25 to 30 minutes. If the oats absorb all the water before they're tender, add more water by the splash and continue to cook until the liquid is absorbed and the grains are soft.

Serve warm, topped with milk, butter, and honey (if desired).

Variations

Granola Oatmeal

Bring the **water** to a boil as directed. When you add the oats and salt, also add **¼ cup coarsely chopped dried fruit**, such as prunes, dates, or apricots, **2 teaspoons flaxseeds**, and **¼ teaspoon ground cinnamon**. Cook the oats over medium-low until they start to thicken, about 10 minutes, then stir in **¼ cup coarsely chopped toasted nuts** (see page 67 for how to toast), such as hazelnuts, walnuts, or almonds. Continue cooking until thickened and tender as directed. Top with a **splash of milk** or spoonful of yogurt.

Golden Milk Oatmeal

Bring only **1 cup water** to a boil. Add the **oats, salt,** and **1 cup whole milk** and cook over medium-low until it starts to thicken, about 10 minutes. Stir in **1 teaspoon vanilla extract, ¼ teaspoon ground turmeric,** and **⅛ teaspoon each cinnamon, cardamom, ginger,** and **black pepper**. Continue cooking until thickened and tender as directed. Top with a **pat of butter** and a **scoop of raw honey.**

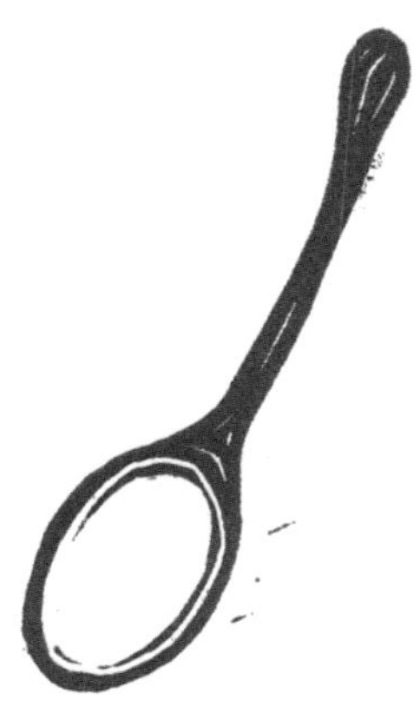

PROBIOTIC GREEN SMOOTHIE

Serves 1

I originally created this smoothie recipe for my superfood business, Golde, and then it became my personal go-to. This recipe uses fiber-rich celery and romaine but still tastes distinctly fruity (a handful of mulberries gives it extra sweetness). I like to add yogurt or kefir for extra protein and fat, which also makes it creamy and filling.

Gluten-free

½ cup water, plus more as needed

3 large leaves romaine lettuce, coarsely chopped

1 celery stalk, coarsely chopped

3 ounces (about ⅔ cup) frozen mango chunks

3 ounces (about ⅔ cup) frozen pineapple chunks

¼ cup whole-milk Greek yogurt or kefir

3 tablespoons dried white mulberries, or 1 pitted Medjool date

2 teaspoons matcha powder

Ice cubes, as needed

In a blender, combine the water, lettuce, celery, mango, pineapple, yogurt, mulberries, and matcha. Blend on high until smooth, adding a couple ice cubes to thicken or more water to thin the smoothie as needed for your desired consistency. Serve immediately.

Variation

Golden Turmeric Smoothie

For a caffeine-free smoothie that tastes delightfully tropical, swap the matcha powder for **½ teaspoon ground turmeric**.

A FRUIT SALAD FOR ALL SEASONS

Each recipe serves 2 to 4

A fruit salad is the flower arrangement of food: Simple, striking combinations will yield delightful results. This is where uniform slices as opposed to haphazard chopping will make a difference: Take your time cutting and always use a very sharp knife. When you've got your fruit ready to go, assemble with care on a plate that you like (it matters).

These salads can be made with any fruit, but abandon thoughts of supermarket versions with mushy melon and sad grapes. Opt for what's in season, right now. Summertime presents a wealth of options, but don't forget that citrus peaks in winter.

These salads shine with the simplest of dressings (just olive oil and salt are a savory foil to the sweet and sour produce). Pears and apples can benefit from a little extra acid from a mild vinegar or citrus juice. Fresh herbs are welcome here, too: Mint is a classic pairing, but play with what a little fresh oregano or tarragon can do. A sprinkle of chopped nuts, like pistachios or walnuts, adds richness in addition to olive oil. These salads are best enjoyed immediately—prep them just prior to serving.

Gluten-free, vegan

Spring

PEPPERED STRAWBERRIES WITH MINT

Place **12 ounces strawberries** (hulled and halved) in a medium bowl and toss with **¼ cup torn mint leaves, 2 tablespoons balsamic vinegar**, and **¼ teaspoon freshly ground black pepper**. Transfer to a serving plate or shallow bowl. Drizzle with **extra-virgin olive oil**, then sprinkle with **flaky sea salt**.

Summer

MIXED STONE FRUIT WITH FRESH OREGANO

Halve **3 small or 2 large plums** and **1 large peach or nectarine** (**or 2 large apricots**). Slice the fruit into ¼-inch wedges, removing the pits as you slice.

Arrange on a serving plate or shallow bowl, and sprinkle with **2 tablespoons fresh oregano or tarragon leaves**. Drizzle with **1 tablespoon apple cider vinegar** (**or fresh lemon or lime juice**) and some **extra-virgin olive oil** over top. Then sprinkle with **flaky sea salt** and **black pepper** or **freshly ground coriander** (use a spice mill or crush the seeds with the back of a spoon). Add more vinegar to taste.

CONTINUED

Fall

RED PEARS AND PERSIMMON WITH WALNUTS

Halve, core, and thinly slice **2 small red Anjou pears**. Trim the stems from **2 Fuyu persimmons**. Halve the fruit (no need to peel), then thinly slice into half-moons.

Lay out half the fruit on a serving plate or shallow bowl. Drizzle with **2 teaspoons of unseasoned rice vinegar or apple cider vinegar**, a bit of **honey** and **extra-virgin olive oil**, and **a pinch of flaky sea salt**. Repeat with the remaining fruit and dressings. Sprinkle over a handful of **chopped toasted walnuts** (see page 67 for how to toast).

NOTE: Look for squat, rounded Fuyu persimmons or Sharon fruit, which can be eaten when firm (as opposed to acorn-shaped Hachiya variations, which must be spoon-ably soft to enjoy).

Winter

PINK LADY APPLES AND CARA CARA ORANGES WITH PISTACHIOS

Working with one piece of citrus at a time, slice a thin piece off the top and bottom off **2 Cara Cara oranges** so they can stand up, then use your knife to slice off the peel and pith in sections from top to bottom. Slice between the membranes running top to bottom of the oranges to remove even segments of fruit. Transfer the wedges to a medium bowl and toss with **a pinch of flaky sea salt**. Set aside. Slice **1 Pink Lady apple** off its core (no need to peel) and cut into ½-inch wedges. Arrange the apples on a serving plate or shallow bowl.

Leaving the citrus juices in the medium bowl for a moment, remove the citrus pieces and arrange around the apples. Pour the accumulated juices over all the fruit. Drizzle with some **extra-virgin olive oil**, then sprinkle with **more flaky sea salt** and a handful of **chopped toasted pistachios** (see page 67 for how to toast).

NOTE: A humble navel orange pairs so well with a good storing apple—I like Pink Ladies and rough-skinned russeted varieties, but anything with "crisp" in the title is a safe bet for texture.

KEEP YOUR ZEST

When you're slicing any citrus, zest it first. I use a Microplane, but any tool that finely grates will work. Leave the zest on a plate and let it dry out completely, which takes a day or so. You can store it in a spice jar and add it on demand (give it a little rub with your fingers to open it up) to season everything from spiced stews to muffin batters.

ISSEY'S BUTTERY OMELET

Serves 1

This is a simple omelet that my husband makes for us often. It's closest to a French omelet, and thanks to the quick cook time, the eggs stay soft and tender. Use a well-seasoned carbon steel or stainless steel pan, which become nonstick when properly heated.

Gluten-free

3 eggs

2 tablespoons unsalted butter

2 tablespoons finely chopped fresh chives

Flaky sea salt and freshly ground black pepper, for serving

In a medium bowl, beat the eggs with a fork until well combined. Heat a medium carbon steel or stainless steel pan over medium-high heat for 1 minute.

Add half of the butter. Let the butter melt, swirling to coat the surface of the pan (it may brown a bit).

Immediately pour the eggs into the pan. Let the eggs just start to set, about 5 seconds, then give the pan a couple of shakes to loosen the eggs from the pan. Use the flat back edge of the fork or a flexible spatula to stir the eggs lightly, allowing the cooked egg curds to separate and the raw runny areas to seep through and continue setting, about 30 more seconds. Once the eggs are mostly set (the surface will look almost matte, as opposed to wet and shiny), sprinkle on the chives.

Tip the pan forward to shimmy the eggs toward the front of the pan. Starting with the edge that's furthest away from you, use the fork or spatula to fold one-third of the omelet over into the center, then fold over the edge that's near the front of the pan. Use the fork or a spatula (or a flick of your wrist holding the skillet) to flip the omelet over so that the seam side is down. Leave to cook for about 10 seconds to seal the seam and finish setting the omelet, then turn off the heat.

Slide the omelet onto a plate, seam-side down. Drag the rest of the butter over the surface, letting it melt on the hot omelet. Sprinkle with salt and pepper and serve.

SERVE WITH

Crispy Breakfast Potatoes (page 92)

Greens for Breakfast (page 80)

Grilled Bread (page 107)

Nuts 'n' Herbs Sauce (page 65)

CRISPY BREAKFAST POTATOES

Serves 4

These breakfast potatoes are also my favorite alongside roast chicken. The secret to the moist interior and crispy texture is using potatoes that have been brine-boiled. They're already cooked through, so you can focus on pan-crisping. It's also a lesson in cooking basics. Don't fret over the pan and stir too often: Giving the potatoes a chance to crisp up properly, undisturbed, in very hot oil is what makes this a success.

Gluten-free, vegan

¼ cup extra-virgin olive oil

1 tablespoon granulated garlic, or 2 teaspoons garlic powder

2 teaspoons smoked paprika, sweet or hot

½ teaspoon ground coriander or cumin

3 cups ½-inch chunks Brine-Boiled Potatoes (page 51; from about 1 pound raw waxy or starchy potatoes)

Flaky sea salt, for serving

In a bowl, whisk together the oil, garlic, smoked paprika, and coriander. Add the potatoes and toss to coat in the oil mixture.

Heat a cast-iron skillet over medium-high heat until you start to see wisps of smoke, 3 to 5 minutes. Add the potatoes and all the spiced oil in a single layer. Let cook, without stirring, until a golden-brown crust begins to form on the bottom of the potatoes, 2 to 3 minutes. Toss the potatoes (a fish spatula is helpful to scrape up and flip) and continue to cook, tossing every 1 to 2 minutes, until they're crispy all over, 5 to 7 more minutes.

Remove from the heat and sprinkle with flaky sea salt. Best eaten immediately.

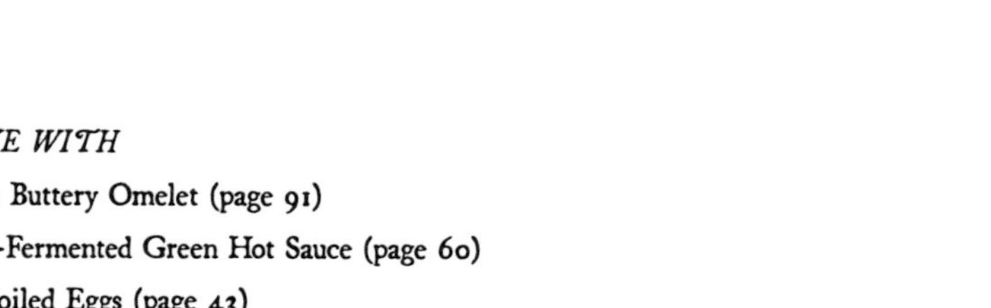

SERVE WITH

Issey's Buttery Omelet (page 91)

Quick-Fermented Green Hot Sauce (page 60)

Soft-Boiled Eggs (page 43)

SOOTHING RICE PORRIDGE

Serves 4

This is a Japanese-style rice porridge known as *okayu*. I ate this every morning in the early weeks of postpartum after my first daughter was born. It's what our family reaches for whenever we need a simple, nourishing dish that warms from the inside out. For the smoothest porridge, let the rice soak in cold water before cooking.

Gluten-free, vegan

---

6 cups water, preferred stock (see $0 Scrap Stock, page 34), or Scallion Trimmings Stock (page 37)

1 cup short-grain rice, washed (see page 45) and soaked if desired (see Notes)

¼ cup dried wakame seaweed (see Notes)

1 tablespoon dried red shiso

Sea salt

Toasted sesame seeds, toasted sesame oil, and/or thinly sliced scallion, for serving

In a large heavy-bottomed pot or donabe, combine the water, rice, wakame, and shiso. Cover with a lid and bring the mixture to a boil over medium-high heat (you'll hear the bubbling). When it comes to a boil, uncover and stir the mixture, making sure that nothing is stuck to the bottom of the pot. Cover again and reduce the heat to low. Continue to cook the porridge (resist the urge to peek) for 30 minutes.

Turn off the heat and let the porridge steam for 10 minutes. Uncover and stir the porridge—the rice grains should be totally cooked through, broken open, and creamy; but the porridge should still be fairly loose.

Season the porridge with salt to taste. Serve bowls of porridge topped with toasted sesame seeds and any other toppings.

NOTES: If you have time, soak the rice, which makes the texture softer and can aid in digestion. Place the washed rice in a bowl, cover with an inch of water, and soak for at least 30 minutes or up to 4 hours. Drain off the excess water before starting the recipe.

This recipe calls for wakame seaweed, which you've probably had in miso soup. You can typically find it dried and ready for use anywhere Asian groceries are available.

SERVE WITH

Gingered Carrots (page 54)

Soft-Boiled Eggs (page 43)

Sweet and Zingy Quick Pickles (page 58)

THE ART OF THE YOGURT BOWL

Each recipe serves 1

This is my most frequent weekday breakfast because it's equal parts effortless and lovely. The key here is to start with a high-quality yogurt. I will always advocate for finding a locally sourced option from a smaller producer, but any whole-milk Greek-style yogurt will do the job. I prefer a strained yogurt because the richer texture holds up more nicely to the toppings.

A yogurt bowl can go sweet or savory: Frozen fruit and honey deliver an almost-dessert experience; peppery extra-virgin olive oil with flaky sea salt is lovely beside morning eggs. My favorite as of late is to have it all: a little honey and olive oil on top of the yogurt, with a side of Grilled Bread (page 107).

Gluten-free

RASPBERRY AND HONEY YOGURT BOWL

Top **1 cup whole-milk Greek yogurt** with **¼ cup fresh or frozen raspberries**. Drizzle generously with **raw honey**. Frozen raspberries will cause the honey to harden into a stringy candy—my favorite part.

MAPLE TAHINI YOGURT BOWL

In a small bowl, whisk together **1 tablespoon maple syrup**, **1 tablespoon tahini**, and **¼ teaspoon ground cinnamon or cardamom**. Swirl into **1 cup whole-milk Greek yogurt** and top with **a pinch of flaky sea salt**.

SALTED SESAME YOGURT BOWL

Top **1 cup whole-milk Greek yogurt** with a **generous drizzle of toasted sesame oil** (or **extra-virgin olive oil**), **1 teaspoon toasted sesame seeds**, and **a pinch of flaky sea salt**.

GREEN HERB YOGURT BOWL

Finely chop about **¼ cup fresh tender herb leaves**, such as parsley, dill, or cilantro. Stir the herbs into **1 cup whole-milk Greek yogurt** and top with **a drizzle of extra-virgin olive oil**, and **a dusting of freshly ground coriander**.

Component-Cooked Breakfast Assemblies

A good breakfast can be as simple as a couple Component-Cooked dishes with a drizzle of good olive oil and a sprinkle of flaky sea salt.

Soft-Boiled Eggs (page 43) + Grilled Bread (page 107) or Easiest Rice (page 44)

Skillet Jam (page 68) + Grilled Bread (page 107)

60:40 Beans (page 38) + Quick-Fermented Green Hot Sauce (page 60)

Baked Whole Sweet Potatoes (page 61) + 1-2-3 Sauce (page 64)

Broth-Simmered Farro (page 48) + any Mix-and-Sit Pickles (page 52)

LUNCH

PAUSE

If you want to do something radical today, take a lunch break. Notice now if you're feeling some twinge of resistance to the idea of breaking in the middle of the day. When we rob ourselves of pause, we miss the opportunity to be here—not out to lunch, but in the human experience. What we uncover in the gap between our to-do lists and news feeds is the juicy reality of our existence, here and now. We taste the tomato and it sings in our ear, simply because today we have chosen to listen. That tune carries through to every interaction we have with our world, adding a little brightness to the flavor of the present moment.

The recipes and techniques in this chapter offer the hopeful argument that a midday pause is very much within reach. You'll find more of my strong opinions on the value of starting with fresh, in-season produce, which makes quickly assembling delicious food massively easier. Thanks to the magic of simple techniques and Component Cooking, most of what you need to put together will already be awaiting you in the fridge.

GREEN BEAN GOMAE

Serves 2

Gomae (pronounced goh-ma-eh) is a homestyle Japanese dish that's won my heart. The simple sauce of sesame seeds, soy sauce, and a touch of sugar can dress any lightly cooked vegetable and make a meal in minutes. It's traditionally served over boiled spinach, but I especially love it over cold green beans.

Vegan option

3 tablespoons toasted sesame seeds (see Note)

2 teaspoons cane sugar

Sea salt

1 tablespoon soy sauce

1 teaspoon fish sauce (optional)

1 pound Brine-Boiled Green Beans (page 51)

Grind the sesame seeds in a small mortar and pestle or in a spice grinder until sandy. Mix in the sugar and a pinch of salt. Mix in the soy sauce until a chunky mixture forms.

Pour over the green beans and toss to coat in the sesame mixture. Season with more salt to taste.

NOTE: Because we enjoy this so often at home, I usually mix up a larger batch of ground toasted sesame seeds (I use a spice grinder or mortar and pestle; see page 67 for how to toast seeds) and sugar in advance, at a ratio of three parts freshly ground sesame seeds to one part cane sugar. I'll add 2 tablespoons of the mixture and 1 tablespoon of soy sauce to the green beans when I'm ready to eat.

SERVE WITH

Easiest Rice (page 44)

Soft-Boiled Eggs (page 43)

Whole-Poached Chicken (page 42)

ROASTED RADISHES AND THEIR GREENS

Serves 4

Overlooked radish tops deserve their time in the spotlight. Too often we chuck out the tops of root vegetables, missing the opportunity to embrace the fact that they are not only edible, but also really delicious. When you're shopping for radishes, go for small (about 1-inch) bulbs and perky-looking greens. Often an oversize red radish is simply overgrown, which yields a bitter flavor and rough texture. I like French breakfast radishes, which are small enough to roast whole. If you use anything larger, slice the bulbs into halves or quarters first. This method also works well with Japanese turnips and small beets.

Gluten-free, vegan option

2 bunches of French breakfast or red radishes with their greens, washed

4 tablespoons extra-virgin olive oil

Sea salt and freshly ground black pepper

2 oil-packed anchovy fillets (optional)

4 garlic cloves, thinly sliced, or 2 teaspoons garlic powder

1 tablespoon apple cider vinegar, plus more to taste

Preheat the oven to 425°F with a sheet pan inside—by the time the oven is preheated, so is your pan.

Remove the leafy tops from the radishes and set them aside. If the radishes are larger than 1 inch, halve them. Transfer the radishes to a medium bowl and toss with 2 tablespoons of the olive oil and a couple big pinches of salt and a few grinds of black pepper.

Remove the preheated baking sheet from the oven and arrange the radishes evenly on top (if they're sliced, position them cut-side down). Return to the oven and roast until the flesh is slightly tender and the skin is slightly blistered and charred in spots, 20 to 25 minutes. Remove from the oven and let cool slightly on the sheet pan.

When the radishes are just about done roasting, in a large skillet, heat the remaining 2 tablespoons olive oil over medium-high heat until it ripples. Add the anchovies (if using) and use a wooden spoon to gently break them up a bit. Add the greens, season with a pinch of salt, and give them a quick stir. Cover the skillet and cook until the leaves have wilted slightly, 3 to 5 minutes.

Uncover the skillet, stir the greens, and sprinkle in the garlic. Cover and cook until the garlic is soft and the greens are totally wilted, another 3 minutes or so.

Transfer the greens to a serving dish and top with the roasted radishes, then drizzle with the vinegar, adding more to taste, and eat immediately.

SERVE WITH

60:40 Beans (page 38)

Soft-Boiled Eggs (page 43)

SHREDDED CHICKEN SALAD WITH YOGURT AND FENNEL

Serves 4

My kind of chicken salad is packed with green herbs and fragrant fennel. By swapping most of the mayo out for yogurt, the result is a lighter dish that lends a brightness to lunchtime.

In a large bowl, whisk together the yogurt, mayonnaise, mustard, garlic, lemon zest, lemon juice, ¼ teaspoon salt, and a few grinds of pepper.

Add the shredded chicken to the bowl with the yogurt mixture along with the fennel, dill, and scallions and stir to combine. Serve immediately, or refrigerate for up to 24 hours so the flavors really meld.

When you're ready to eat, season to taste with more salt and pepper. Serve with tender greens and grilled bread (see below).

NOTE: **If your fennel has the fronds attached, use them in the salad in addition to the dill. Save the fibrous stalks for $0 Scrap Stock** **(page 34)****.**

Gluten-free

¼ cup whole-milk Greek yogurt

2 tablespoons mayonnaise

2 tablespoons Dijon mustard

1 garlic clove, finely grated

1 tablespoon grated lemon zest (from 1 lemon)

3 tablespoons fresh lemon juice (from 1 lemon)

Sea salt and freshly ground black pepper

2 cups shredded chicken breast (from Whole Poached Chicken, page 42), skin removed

1 small fennel bulb (see Note), finely chopped

⅔ cup finely chopped fresh dill (leaves and tender stems)

2 scallions, thinly sliced

Tender greens and grilled bread, for serving

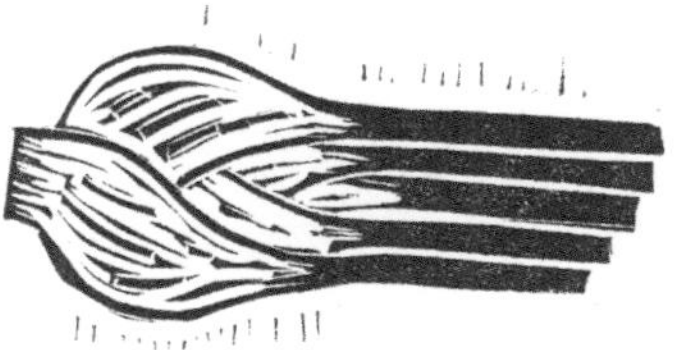

GRILLED BREAD

A slice of crusty sourdough bread is one of my favorite accompaniments to a simple meal—and so much more satisfying than toast. I use a Japanese-style grill net that goes over the top of my gas stove, grilling the bread on both sides until charred. If you don't have a grill net, make this in the broiler: Heat the broiler on high and let the bread grill until charred, 1 to 3 minutes per side. All broilers have different strengths, so keep an eye on your bread the whole time to prevent burning. Drizzle with olive oil and top with flaky sea salt for serving.

CHUNKY SALADS

Each recipe serves 4

I prefer a salad that's got big chunks of vegetables that have loads of texture and flavor over the underwhelming leafy green variety. The beautiful thing about a chunky salad is you're really just letting the ingredients sing through—no complicated dressings and tiny whisks needed. Focus on embracing what's in season and really good, right now. That means celebrating tender spring peas and turnips, while you await summer's sweetest tomatoes. Luckily for those of us with long falls and winters, I've found that the smaller, Persian-style cucumbers are pretty consistently delicious. Follow The Chunky Salad Formula with any veg you have, or plan for one of the following recipes. I love to grab a few Soft-Boiled Eggs (page 43) and some good sourdough bread to eat alongside.

The Chunky Salad Formula

Chop your veg

I like one or two options for flavor and texture, using about 1½ pounds total

Tomatoes, big wedges of heirloom tomato or halved cherry tomatoes

Corn kernels, cut off the cob

Cucumber, coarsely chopped

Turnip, sliced. The small Hakurei variety are sweetest, but peeled Purple Top White Globes are also great raw

Radishes, quartered if small, or sliced thin if they're big spicy varieties

Fennel, sliced

Brine-Boiled Veg (page 50), such as green beans, potatoes, or cauliflower also work well

Add herbs and aromatics

Large-leaved tender herbs, such as basil, mint, shiso. Thinly slice leaves into ribbons or roughly tear

Other tender herbs, such as parsley, cilantro, dill, tarragon. Roughly chop or tear—leaves and tender stems are edible

Woody herb leaves, such as oregano, marjoram, thyme. Leave whole or coarsely chop—a little goes a long way

Garlic (a clove or two), ½ onion, a shallot, or a few scallions. Use a sharp paring knife or mandoline for paper-thin slices

Add a crunch

Top with a handful of **sesame seeds, walnuts, hazelnuts, or pistachios**, toasted (see page 67) and finely chopped

Sprinkle with

Seeds, such as fennel seed, coriander seed, cumin seed, coarsely ground black or pink peppercorns

Dress it up

Use one oil and one vinegar along with extras as desired to dress the salad. There's no need for an emulsified vinaigrette, just drizzle over the produce and toss to combine

Oil: extra-virgin olive oil for grassy floral richness, toasted sesame oil for light nuttiness

Vinegar: apple cider vinegar for light fruity tang, red wine vinegar for punchier fruitiness, rice vinegar (seasoned or unseasoned) for mild sweetness, balsamic for robust sweetness, black vinegar for smoky-sweet tang

For umami salty, savory notes: fish sauce or soy sauce

For sweetness: maple syrup or honey

Add a salty bite

Olives, oil-cured, chopped or sliced

Capers, salt-cured (rinsed) or brined

Anchovies, oil-packed, coarsely chopped

Flaky sea salt: Always finish your salad with a pinch or two of flaky sea salt, adding more to taste. Getting used to informal salting helps to build confidence in understanding how flavor works, and firms up your personal preferences

CONTINUED

Spring

ASPARAGUS AND SNAP PEAS WITH LEMON AND MINT

Gluten-free, vegan

Slice **1 pound Brine-Boiled Asparagus** (page 51) on the bias into 1-inch pieces. Thinly slice **½ pound sugar snap peas** on the bias. Place the veg in a large bowl, then toss with **½ cup fresh mint leaves**, the **finely grated zest and juice of 1 lemon, 2 tablespoons olive oil**, then season with **flaky sea salt and freshly ground black pepper** to taste. When you're ready to serve, sprinkle with **¼ cup chopped toasted hazelnuts or walnuts** (see page 67).

Summer

HEIRLOOM TOMATO AND SWEET CORN

Gluten-free, vegan

Use a paring knife to cut out the cores from **1 pound heirloom tomatoes (about 2 large)**. Slice the tomatoes into 1-inch wedges and arrange on a large serving plate. Sprinkle with **flaky sea salt.**

Shuck **2 ears of corn**, then halve each cob crosswise. Working with one half at a time, slice the corn kernels off each. (Save the spent cobs for $0 Scrap Stock, page 34.) Sprinkle the corn kernels all over the tomatoes.

Slice **1 stalk spring garlic** (or **2 scallions**) as thinly as you possibly can, then scatter over the top. Drizzle with **red wine vinegar or apple cider vinegar** and **extra-virgin olive oil**, then sprinkle with more **flaky sea salt** and **freshly ground coriander seed or black pepper**.

NOTE: In the summertime when tomatoes and sweet corn are at their peak, I love to use all raw ingredients, especially fresh garlic (sometimes known as spring garlic), which has a milder flavor than the paper-y cured garlic you can find year-round. Check the farmers' market for fresh garlic, but if you can't find it, use scallions instead.

WAIT FOR THE BEST TOMATOES

Please (!) wait until tomato season—that's the middle of summertime through early fall—to start digging in. When in season, dozens of varieties are plentiful at the market. Enjoy them fresh while you can and then kiss them good-bye until next year. Canned tomatoes are great year-round for sauces, soups, and stews.

Always store fresh tomatoes at room temperature: Putting them in the fridge makes the flavor bland. Store big tomatoes "shoulders down" and uncovered on your counter; store little ones in a colander so the whole pile can breathe. If they need to ripen, leave them in a sunny spot until they smell fragrant and feel heavy.

CONTINUED

Fall

SNOW PEA AND HAKUREI TURNIP WITH SESAME AND SOY

Gluten-free, vegan

Prep **1 pound snow peas** by snapping off the stem ends and peeling off the fibrous strands. Roughly chop and transfer to a large bowl. Trim the greens from **½ pound Hakurei turnips or red radishes** (save them for Greens for Breakfast, page 80), scrub clean, and chop into ½-inch wedges. Thinly slice **2 large scallions**. Toss together in a large bowl.

Lightly drizzle the veg with **soy sauce** and **toasted sesame oil**. Sprinkle with **toasted sesame seeds** and **a pinch of flaky sea salt**.

SERVE WITH

Grilled Bread (page 107)

Shredded Chicken Salad with Yogurt and Fennel (page 107)

Soft-Boiled Eggs (page 43)

Winter

TANGY CRUSHED CUCUMBER WITH SHISO

Gluten-free, vegan (without fish sauce)

Cut **1½ pounds cucumbers (about 2 English or 8 Persian)** into 1-inch irregular chunks, then use the flat of the knife turned on its side or a rolling pin to smash them fairly flat. Place the cucumbers in a colander, toss with **1½ teaspoons sea salt**, and let sit for 10 minutes to draw out the water. Use a towel to wipe off the salt, then squeeze the cucumber with your hands to draw out the excess water. Transfer to a serving bowl.

Drizzle with **rice vinegar or black vinegar** and **extra-virgin olive oil or toasted sesame oil**, then sprinkle with about **¼ cup thinly sliced or torn fresh shiso** (or **2 teaspoons crushed dried shiso**), and more **salt to taste**. A very light drizzle of **fish sauce** is also a great addition. If you'd like, sprinkle with **toasted sesame seeds** before serving.

BITTER GREENS WITH BLACK VINEGAR

Serves 4

I know the word "bitter" can be a little unnerving, but don't let it keep you from giving this recipe a try. Cooking bitter greens—especially broccoli rabe or Italian dandelion greens if you can find them—in butter at a high heat lends a sweetly caramelized flavor that's nicely balanced by the smoky vinegar "dressing."

Gluten-free

---

1 pound broccoli rabe or dandelion greens

½ pound chicories, such as radicchio or escarole

3 tablespoons unsalted butter

2 tablespoons extra-virgin olive oil

2 teaspoons fennel or cumin seeds (optional)

Sea salt and freshly ground black pepper

3 tablespoons black vinegar or balsamic vinegar, plus more to taste

Tear or chop the greens and chicories into bite-size pieces.

In a large skillet, heat the butter, oil, and fennel seeds (if using) over medium-high heat. When the butter is melted, add half the vegetables. Season with a few pinches of salt and pepper and toss to coat everything in the fat. Let the vegetables cook until just starting to wilt and char in places, 3 to 5 minutes. Add the remaining vegetables, toss to combine, and let cook until wilted, another 3 to 5 minutes.

Add the vinegar to the skillet and toss the vegetables to coat. Remove from the heat. Season with more salt, pepper, and vinegar to taste.

NOTE: **Black vinegar is a savory, smoky Chinese vinegar that lends a richer flavor that pairs well with the caramelized greens. If you don't have it on hand, try balsamic vinegar; or apple cider vinegar or red wine vinegar for a lighter, brighter dish.**

SERVE WITH

Easiest Rice (page 44)

Soft-Boiled Eggs (page 43)

BALSAMIC TUNA WITH CHOPPED VEG

Serves 4

There are two keys to making my ideal tuna salad: (1) swapping some of the mayonnaise out for a sweet and tangy vinegar, and (2) mixing in a hefty ratio of crunchy chopped veg. Make sure to use tuna canned in oil, not water, for the best flavor and silkiest texture fish.

Gluten-free

¼ cup balsamic vinegar

2 tablespoons extra-virgin olive oil, plus more for drizzling

1 tablespoon Dijon mustard

1 tablespoon mayonnaise

Two 5-ounce cans oil-packed tuna

1 small red onion, very finely chopped

1 celery stalk, very finely chopped

1 Persian (mini) cucumber or ¼ English cucumber, very finely chopped

1 small carrot, peeled and very finely chopped

½ teaspoon caraway or celery seeds

Sea salt and freshly ground black pepper

In a medium bowl, use a fork to stir together the vinegar, olive oil, mustard, and mayonnaise until smooth.

Pour the tuna and its oil into the bowl with the vinaigrette. Use the fork to flake the tuna into smaller pieces (but not smashing it fully).

Stir in the onion, celery, cucumber, carrot, and caraway seeds. Season with salt and pepper to taste, drizzle with more olive oil before serving.

SERVE WITH

Tender greens

Grilled Bread (page 107)

HOW TO BUY BALSAMIC

Balsamic vinegar varies widely in flavor, cost, and quality. Traditional balsamic vinegar is aged for upward of twelve years—at least twenty-five years for "extra-vecchio," or the most matured—and is viscous and sweet. The longer the aging time, the more expensive the vinegar. I recommend opting for a middle-of-the-road option that has some body and sweetness to it, but isn't so precious that you'll never use it. Avoid balsamic glazes, which are cheaper but usually have added sugar and color to mimic a well-aged vinegar.

HOUSE NIÇOISE

Serves 2

This riff on classic French Niçoise salad is where you really see Component Cooking shine. Having already cooked veg and eggs, jars of homemade pickles, and a well-stocked pantry means I can toss together this salad in less than 10 minutes. Make extra vinaigrette—it lasts in the fridge for about a week, and without the shallot, it'll stay fresh in an airtight container for even longer.

Gluten-free

VINAIGRETTE

1 small shallot, very finely chopped

¼ cup apple cider vinegar, plus more to taste

1 tablespoon Dijon mustard

1 teaspoon maple syrup

½ teaspoon ground coriander

Sea salt and freshly ground black pepper

⅓ cup extra-virgin olive oil

SALAD

1 cup quartered small tomatoes or radishes, sliced cucumbers, or a mix

1 cup Gingered Carrots (page 54), Purple Cabbage Curtido (page 57), or Sweet and Zingy Quick Pickles (page 58)

1 cup halved or quartered Brine-Boiled Potatoes (page 51)

1 cup Brine-Boiled Green Beans (page 51)

2 Soft-Boiled Eggs (page 43), peeled and halved

One 4- or 5-ounce tin oil-packed sardines, mackerel, or tuna

3 ounces Parmesan cheese, thickly sliced (optional)

Flaky sea salt

Make the vinaigrette: In a medium bowl, whisk together the shallot, vinegar, mustard, maple syrup, coriander, a big pinch of salt, and a few grinds of pepper. Slowly whisk in the olive oil until the mixture emulsifies.

Assemble the salad: On a large platter, assemble the vegetables, eggs, and fish in little mounds. Top with the cheese, if using. Drizzle half of the dressing over everything. Sprinkle the fresh veg and eggs with flaky sea salt. Serve with the remaining dressing on the side.

GOLDEN VEGGIE PANCAKES

Makes 10 to 12 pancakes

Savory pancakes are great to make in a big batch when you have free time, and then reheat on-demand for lunch. Opting for golden beets lends a lighter, less earthy flavor, but this works with classic red beets, too.

1 large or 2 small golden beets, scrubbed and peeled

1 medium Yukon Gold potato, scrubbed

1 large carrot, scrubbed

1 medium yellow onion

1¼ teaspoons sea salt

1⅔ cups all-purpose flour

1 tablespoon cumin seeds

1 teaspoon ground turmeric

½ teaspoon ground ginger

1¼ cups water

1 egg

Extra-virgin olive oil, for frying

Line a medium bowl with a kitchen towel. Grate the vegetables on the coarse holes of a box grater and place in the towel-lined bowl. Toss the vegetables with 1 teaspoon of the salt and let sit for 5 minutes. Gather the towel around the vegetables and squeeze to remove as much liquid from the mixture as possible. Let sit for 5 minutes, then repeat two or three more times, until the mixture feels almost dry to the touch.

In another medium bowl, whisk together the flour, cumin seeds, remaining ½ teaspoon salt, the turmeric, and ginger. Make a well in the center and add the water and egg. Whisk until just combined. Fold in the grated veg mixture.

In a large cast-iron skillet, heat 2 tablespoons olive oil over medium-high heat until it ripples.

Scoop two ¼-cupfuls of batter into the pan. Use a fork to spread the batter out to be about 4 inches wide.

Cook until the top of the pancake is starting to look matte, 3 to 4 minutes. Flip the pancake and cook on the second side until deeply golden on the second side, another 2 to 3 minutes. Transfer the pancake(s) to a large plate. If you're going to eat them when all the pancakes are cooked, keep them warm on a sheet pan in a 325°F oven.

Cook the remaining pancakes with the remaining batter, adding more oil as needed to the pan with each batch.

NOTE: If you have any discard from sourdough starter (see page 162 for more on this), you can swap it in for some of the flour and water. Starter is equal parts flour and water, so reduce dry flour and fresh water accordingly.

SERVE WITH

1-2-3 Sauce (page 64)

Nuts 'n' Herbs Sauce (page 65)

Sweet and Zingy Quick Pickles (page 58)

Soft-Boiled Eggs (page 43)

FLUFFY POTATO SALAD

Serves 4

Inspired by Japanese-style potato salad, this has a light, fluffy texture and crunchy vegetables, and is frankly addictive. The key to getting the right texture here is to use hot potatoes—this is a great use for reheated Brine-Boiled Potatoes (page 51).

Gluten-free

2 Persian (mini) cucumbers or ½ English cucumber, quartered lengthwise and thinly sliced

2 scallions, thinly sliced

1 small carrot, peeled, halved lengthwise, and thinly sliced into half-moons

Sea salt

2½ tablespoons mayonnaise

1½ tablespoons unseasoned rice vinegar

1½ teaspoons Dijon or grainy mustard

3 cups ½-inch pieces Brine-Boiled Potatoes (page 51; from about 1 pound raw), such as Russet

Freshly ground black pepper

In a colander, toss the cucumbers, scallions, and carrot with 2 teaspoons salt. Set aside for 10 minutes.

In a small bowl, whisk together the mayonnaise, rice vinegar, and mustard. If you have fresh Brine-Boiled Potatoes, toss them in the mayonnaise dressing in a medium bowl while they are still warm. If the boiled potatoes are cold from the refrigerator, warm them in a saucepan with a splash of water over medium heat, or in the microwave until steaming and heated through, before combining with the dressing. The potatoes should start to smash a bit, but not go totally smooth.

Give the vegetables a rinse to remove excess salt, then shake off the excess water. Stir the vegetables into the potato mixture, then season with more salt and black pepper to taste before serving.

NOTES: I always use Japanese Kewpie mayonnaise because it's made with a blend of flavorful vinegars and just uses egg yolks instead of whole eggs. If you're using another brand, you may want to add a little more rice vinegar to taste.

Fresh raw corn kernels or shelled peas can be swapped in for the cucumber and/or carrot for a taste of summer. Use ½ cup for each sub.

SERVE WITH

Tender greens

Whole Poached Chicken (page 42)

SOFT SQUASH WITH BROWN BUTTER–HAZELNUT DRESSING

Serves 2

Brown butter sauce doesn't sound like it fits into a speedy lunch prep, but it comes together in just 5 minutes. This nutty, golden-hued dish starts with Component-Cooked roasted winter squash (kabocha, acorn, and honeynut roast up especially soft and sweet). It's great with sweet potatoes and carrots, too.

Gluten-free

3 cups 2-inch pieces roasted winter squash (see The Perfect Sheet Pan Veg, page 62)

5 tablespoons unsalted butter

¼ cup finely chopped toasted hazelnuts (see Note)

1 tablespoon grated lemon zest (from 1 large lemon)

2 tablespoons whole-grain or Dijon mustard

3 tablespoons fresh lemon juice (from 1 large lemon)

1 teaspoon maple syrup

Sea salt and freshly ground black pepper

Reheat the squash in a 350°F oven until warmed through, about 10 minutes; or let come to room temperature.

In a small saucepan, melt the butter over medium heat. Whisking often, continue to cook until the butter starts foaming, then turns golden brown and smells nutty, 4 to 6 minutes. It will seem like nothing is happening at first, but don't walk away—the butter can go from browned to burnt in seconds. Immediately pour the brown butter into a heatproof bowl, making sure to scrape in all the toasted bits from the pot.

Stir the nuts and lemon zest into the brown butter. Let sizzle, then cool for 5 minutes. Stir in the mustard, lemon juice, and maple syrup until smooth. Season with salt and pepper to taste.

Place the squash on a serving plate. Pour the warm dressing over the squash and serve.

NOTE: **I like to buy raw hazelnuts and roast them myself (see page 67). Walnuts, almonds, pecans, cashews, and pistachios all swap in well.**

SERVE WITH

Easiest Rice (page 44)

Broth-Simmered Farro (page 48)

Quick-Fermented Green Hot Sauce (page 60)

Component-Cooked Lunch Assemblies

The following ideas are lunches made entirely of recipes from the Component Cooking chapter (page 32) or one of this chapter's recipes plus a Component-Cooked element. Use them as a jumping-off point to find your favorite combinations.

Simple Garlic Chickpeas (page 41) + Garlic and Parsley Butter Rice (page 47)

Balsamic Tuna with Chopped Veg (page 115) + Brine-Boiled Potatoes (page 51)

Whole Poached Chicken (page 42) + 1-2-3 Yogurt Sauce (page 64) + Sweet and Zingy Quick Pickles (page 58)

Broth-Simmered Farro (page 48) + The Perfect Sheet Pan Veg (page 62)

Baked Whole Sweet Potatoes (page 61, made with a Japanese sweet potato) + Gingered Carrots (page 54) + Easiest Rice (page 44)

Green Bean Gomae (page 103) + Easiest Rice (page 44)

Fluffy Potato Salad (page 120) + Soft-Boiled Eggs (page 43) + Sweet and Zingy Quick Pickles (page 58)

Baked Whole Sweet Potatoes (page 61) + 1-2-3 Yogurt Sauce or 1-2-3 Tahini Sauce (page 64)

Broth-Simmered Farro (page 48) + Nuts 'n' Herbs Sauce (page 65)

The Perfect Sheet Pan Veg (page 62) + Sage and Oregano White Beans (page 41)

Bitter Greens with Black Vinegar (page 114) + 60:40 Beans (page 38)

Whole Poached Chicken (page 42) + Nuts 'n' Herbs Sauce (page 65)

Roasted Radishes and Their Greens (page 104) + Soft-Boiled Eggs (page 43)

だし醤油
ANCHOVIES
ANCHOVIES

THE EASE

OF DINNER

I don't often plan weeknight meals in advance. When the clock hits 5 p.m., the first question I ask is, "What do I already have, and how can it become dinner?" I like to rely on a steady rotation of pantry and produce staples that can always create a good meal. Dried pastas, polenta, and rice can easily be combined with Component-Cooked vegetables, beans, or leftover chicken. Most of these recipes take 45 minutes or less—anything a little longer is mostly passive cooking time, which gives you space to attend to your other priorities.

Remember: You have good taste. Don't let apprehension over your own cooking prowess keep you from trusting your authority on what's good. Knife skills are acquired with practice, but picking up on flavors and textures requires only an open mind. Start to see every meal you put together as an experiment. Make observations as you assemble ingredients, cook the food, and then take the first bite. Does it need more salt? Add some now. If that still doesn't quite work, you still have food on the table to explore with. (Does it need some brightness from a splash of vinegar? Richness from a drizzle of olive oil? Maybe next time you'll add paprika for a touch of smokiness.) Now you have the perspective that only comes from experience. Taste your way through the process, and don't rush to condemn yourself for making a mistake. What you're doing now is *learning*, and building up confidence to cook food just the way you like it.

LEFTOVER CHICKEN AND MUSHROOM DONABE RICE

Serves 4

One of my favorite uses for leftover chicken is to cook it with rice. This method simultaneously infuses the rice with rich flavor and gives the meat a moist, fall-apart texture for a no-fail, very filling, one-pot meal. This is made in a donabe, a traditional Japanese clay pot (see page 47). If you don't have one, don't worry—you can still make this in another heavy-bottomed pot. This recipe uses a mix of mushrooms to round out the dish, but you could also use thinly sliced zucchini or hearty greens, such as kale.

2 cups short-grain white rice

3 cups preferred stock (see $0 Scrap Stock, page 34) or water

3 tablespoons soy sauce

2 tablespoons shiro dashi (see Note)

1-inch knob fresh ginger, peeled and thinly sliced

1 teaspoon dried red shiso (optional)

4 scallions or 1 small yellow onion, thinly sliced

4 ounces mixed wild mushrooms, such as oyster, shiitake, and enoki, torn into bite-size pieces or thinly sliced (about 1½ cups)

1 pound bone-in cooked chicken (from Whole Poached Chicken, page 42, or Weeknight Roast Chicken Dinner, page 138)

2 tablespoons unsalted butter, cut into small pieces

Rinse the rice (see page 45) and add to a 2½- to 3-quart donabe or 10-inch heavy-bottomed pot, such as a Dutch oven. Place your index finger on top of the rice. Pour in the stock until it reaches the first knuckle of your index finger (you may not use it all).

Stir in the soy sauce, dashi, ginger, and shiso (if using). Scatter in the scallions and mushrooms. Nestle in the chicken and dot the butter over the top. Cover the donabe or pot.

Set over medium heat and cook for 15 minutes, until you hear faint sizzling. Turn off the heat and let steam for another 15 minutes (don't peek).

Remove the chicken to a plate or cutting board. Stir together the rice mixture until combined. Shred the meat using two forks, discarding the bones. Spoon the rice into bowls and top with the shredded chicken.

NOTE: If you don't have shiro dashi, see "In Place of Shiro Dashi" (page 79) for a pantry-friendly alternative.

SERVE WITH

Quick-Fermented Green Hot Sauce (page 60)

SESAME SOBA NOODLE SALAD

Serves 4

I first came to love soba noodles when celebrating New Year's Eve with my husband's family. (It's a Japanese tradition to eat soba noodles on the holiday to symbolize a long life.) Soba is made with buckwheat flour, which gives the noodles a distinctly nutty flavor and firm texture. I find myself craving them in hot soup every winter and in cold salads year-round. Here they're served with a tahini-miso sauce and scrunched cabbage, with cucumber for crunch, but try swapping in asparagus or carrot if you have them.

Vegan

---

1 pound (½ small head) napa cabbage, very thinly sliced

Sea salt

¼ cup tahini

1 tablespoon white or red miso

1 tablespoon toasted sesame oil or extra-virgin olive oil

3 tablespoons soy sauce, plus more to taste

2 teaspoons garlic powder

1 teaspoon cane sugar

1 (9-ounce) package soba noodles

3 Persian (mini) cucumbers or ½ English cucumber, julienned

5 scallions, thinly sliced

3 tablespoons unseasoned rice vinegar

Toasted sesame seeds, for serving

Bring a medium pot of water to a boil over high heat.

In a medium bowl, combine the cabbage and a couple pinches of salt and use your fingers to scrunch the mixture together until the cabbage is slightly softened. Set aside.

In a small bowl, whisk together the tahini, toasted sesame oil, miso, 1 tablespoon of the soy sauce, the garlic powder, and sugar until smooth. The mixture should be thick.

Add the soba to the boiling water and cook according to the package directions. Just before the noodles are done, scoop out about 1 cup of the noodle cooking water into a mug or liquid measuring cup. Drain the noodles into a colander and rinse with cold water.

Slowly whisk in ¼ cup of the reserved noodle cooking water to the tahini mixture—it should lighten in color and loosen in texture.

Return the rinsed noodles to the pot (off the heat). Scrape the tahini sauce into the pot with the noodles. Use tongs to toss until the noodles are totally coated with the sauce.

Drain any excess liquid from the scrunched cabbage. Add the cucumbers, scallions, vinegar, and remaining 2 tablespoons soy sauce to the cabbage and toss to coat. Set aside about one-quarter of the mixture.

Add the remaining vegetable mixture to the noodles and toss to coat, adding more noodle cooking water by the splash as needed if the mixture seems at all dry (you may not use all the water). Taste and season with more soy sauce.

Serve the saucy noodles garnished with the reserved vegetable mixture, as well as the sesame seeds.

CURRIED LENTIL STEW

Serves 4

This is a simple warming stew that's made very easy with Component-Cooked vegetables. I like to serve it with a dollop of yogurt to temper the spice, but a final drizzle of olive oil and a bit of chopped parsley would be lovely, too.

Gluten-free, vegan

¼ cup extra-virgin olive oil

2 medium carrots or 3 celery stalks, finely chopped

1 large onion, coarsely chopped

Sea salt

3 garlic cloves, thinly sliced

2 teaspoons ground turmeric

2 teaspoons ground cumin

2 teaspoons fennel seeds

1 teaspoon yellow mustard seeds

½ teaspoon red pepper flakes

1½ cups lentils, rinsed

4 cups preferred stock (see $0 Scrap Stock, page 34)

2 cups coarsely chopped Brine-Boiled Cauliflower or White Potatoes (page 51; from about ¾ pound raw) or Baked Whole Sweet Potatoes (page 61)

3 cups water

In a large heavy-bottomed pot, heat the oil over medium heat until it ripples. Stir in the carrots and onion with a pinch of salt. Cook, stirring often, until the veg has softened a bit, 5 to 8 minutes. Stir in the garlic, turmeric, cumin, fennel seeds, mustard seeds, and red pepper flakes. Let cook until fragrant, about 1 minute.

Stir in the lentils, stock, cauliflower, and water. Add another big pinch of salt and increase the heat to medium-high. Let the mixture come to a boil. Reduce the heat to medium-low, partially cover, and cook until the lentils are cooked through and starting to break open, and the liquid has reduced a bit, 30 to 40 minutes.

Season the stew with more salt to taste and serve.

SERVE WITH

Easiest Rice (page 44)

Nuts 'n' Herbs Sauce (page 65)

Quick-Fermented Green Hot Sauce (page 60)

"INSTANT" ANY-VEG SOUP

Serves 4

One of my favorite weeknight cooking tricks is throwing a good premade stock over any vegetables to make an (almost) instant soup. Using Component-Cooked brine-boiled veg makes the process even faster, but you can use 1½ pounds of finely chopped raw vegetables, too (just account for an extra 7 to 10 minutes of cooking time). This is a great vehicle for leftover Whole Poached Chicken (page 42) or 60:40 Beans (page 38), and any fresh greens that are on their way out, too. Stir those in at the end until warmed through.

Gluten-free, vegan

¼ cup extra-virgin olive oil, plus more for drizzling

1 large yellow or red onion, coarsely chopped

Sea salt and freshly ground black pepper

2 teaspoons ground cumin or coriander

4 cups coarsely chopped Brine-Boiled Veg (page 50, from about 1½ pounds raw), such as zucchini or summer squash, carrot, winter squash, sweet potato, cauliflower, or broccoli

4 cups preferred stock (see $0 Scrap Stock, page 34)

8 ounces greens, such as kale, Swiss chard, spinach, or dandelion greens, roughly torn (optional)

1 tablespoon apple cider vinegar or lemon juice

In a large heavy-bottomed pot, heat the oil over medium-high heat. When it starts to ripple, add the onion, a pinch of salt, and a few grinds of pepper. Cook, stirring occasionally, until just starting to brown, 5 to 8 minutes. Add the cumin and let sizzle for 30 seconds, until fragrant, then add the brine-boiled vegetables. Season with another pinch of salt and more black pepper.

Add the stock, increase the heat to high, and bring the mixture to a boil. Reduce the heat to medium and let simmer for 10 minutes, until the flavors have melded. When you're ready to serve, turn off the heat and stir in the greens, if using (they'll wilt in the hot soup), and vinegar. Season with more salt and pepper to taste.

Serve with a drizzle of olive oil.

SERVE WITH

Cooked noodles/pasta or toast

Broth-Simmered Farro (page 48)

Easiest Rice (page 44)

ROASTED VEG OVER TOASTED CORIANDER POLENTA

Serves 4

Polenta has the charm of making a simple weeknight dinner feel a little elegant. This recipe works with any sheet pan veg, but I especially love it with broccoli rabe. Coriander is my favorite cooking spice for savory dishes, because it adds a floral, citrus note wherever it's added.

Gluten-free

---

2 tablespoons coriander seeds (see Note)

3 cups whole milk

3 cups water, plus more as needed

1 cup polenta (not instant)

Sea salt

4 cups cut-up The Perfect Sheet Pan Veg (page 62), such as broccoli, carrots, or summer squash

½ cup finely grated Parmesan cheese (optional)

3 tablespoons unsalted butter

2 tablespoons fresh lemon juice

Heat a large pot over medium heat. Add the coriander and toast, shaking the pan frequently, until the seeds are very fragrant, 30 seconds to 1 minute. Pour out into a small bowl to cool. Once cool, finely grind in a mortar and pestle or spice grinder.

Add the milk and water to the pot, increase the heat to medium-high, and bring to a boil. Whisk in the polenta and ½ teaspoon salt and bring to a simmer (you should see small bubbles). Reduce the heat to low, cover the pot, and continue to cook, whisking every 10 minutes or so, until the polenta is tender and creamy, like a loose porridge, 25 to 35 minutes. As it cools it will continue to thicken, so err on the side of a looser mixture.

Meanwhile, reheat the veg in a 350°F oven until warmed through, about 10 minutes.

When the polenta is cooked through, give it a whisk and add more water as needed to loosen to your desired texture. Turn off the heat and stir in the ground toasted coriander, Parmesan (if using), and butter. Season with more salt to taste.

Drizzle the lemon juice over the warm veg, then serve over the polenta.

NOTE: **If you don't have whole coriander seeds, use 2 teaspoons whole black peppercorns, toasted according to the recipe; or 1 tablespoon ground coriander, toasted for 15 to 30 seconds.**

SERVE WITH

60:40 Beans (page 38), warmed

Nuts 'n' Herbs Sauce (page 65)

Soft-Boiled Eggs (page 43)

Whole Poached Chicken (page 42)

ONE-POT BROCCOLI PASTA

Serves 4

I make this when I want "restaurant pasta," but am short on time and ingredients. It's a lovely Italian-inspired meal that you never knew could come from your home kitchen. Using one pot for the broccoli and the pasta makes for a breezy cleanup before bed—*almost* as simple as ordering in.

1½ pounds broccoli with the stalks (about 2 medium heads)

Sea salt

12 ounces short pasta, such as orecchiette, cavatelli, or penne

4 large garlic cloves, finely chopped, or 2 teaspoons garlic powder

⅓ cup extra-virgin olive oil

1 cup coarsely chopped walnuts or blanched hazelnuts

½ teaspoon freshly ground black pepper, plus more to taste

2 tablespoons chopped fresh oregano, or 2 teaspoons dried

¼ cup finely grated Parmesan cheese, plus more for serving

1 lemon

½ cup finely chopped fresh parsley

Bring a large pot of water to a boil over high heat.

While that's heating up, use a paring knife to slice the broccoli florets from the head into ½-inch pieces directly into a colander. (I don't bother using a cutting board for this part—it just makes a mess.)

Use a vegetable peeler to remove the tough outer skin from the broccoli stems, trim off the bottom, then roughly chop and add to the colander with the florets.

When the pot of water comes to a boil, add 3 tablespoons sea salt (salt generously to season both the pasta and broccoli). Stir in the pasta, garlic, and three-quarters of the broccoli. Set a timer according to the pasta package directions for al dente. Just before draining, scoop out 2 cups of the cooking water into a mug or liquid measuring cup and set aside. Drain the pasta, garlic, and broccoli into a colander over the remaining broccoli.

Return the empty pot to the stove over medium-low heat for a minute to dry out. Add the oil and nuts, then increase the heat to medium. Stirring often, toast the nuts until fragrant and deeply golden, 3 to 5 minutes.

Stir in the black pepper and oregano. Let sizzle until fragrant, about 30 seconds. Stir in the pasta, garlic, and broccoli. Turn off the heat. Add the Parmesan and ½ cup of reserved pasta water. Stir vigorously for 1 to 2 minutes, adding more pasta water by the splash, until the pasta is glossy (you may not use all the water).

Grate the zest of the lemon right into the pot, then halve the lemon and juice half into the pot. Add the parsley and stir to combine. Season with more lemon juice, salt, and pepper to taste.

Top servings with more Parmesan and the toasted nuts.

WEEKNIGHT ROAST CHICKEN DINNER

Serves 4

The secret to making roast chicken a weeknight reality is using a small bird, and roasting it hot and fast. This recipe works best if you salt the chicken a day ahead of time, which helps the skin crisp up nicely and distributes flavor throughout the meat. I highly recommend pouring the warm chicken drippings from the pan over rice.

Gluten-free

---

1 small whole chicken (about 3 pounds)

2 teaspoons sea salt

1 tablespoon extra-virgin olive oil

1½ teaspoons freshly ground black pepper

Easiest Rice (page 44), for serving

Brine-Boiled Veg (page 50), for serving

NOTE: If you're short on time, season the chicken 30 minutes in advance, letting it sit at room temperature until it goes in the oven.

Place the chicken on a sheet pan or large plate. Remove any giblets from the cavity, then pat the chicken dry with paper towels. Season all over with the salt. Refrigerate, uncovered, for up to 24 hours (see Note). Remove the chicken from the fridge 30 minutes before roasting.

Place a large (at least 12-inch) ovenproof skillet on the center rack of the oven and preheat the oven to 450°F with the skillet inside.

Pat the chicken dry (salt draws out moisture). Drizzle the olive oil all over the chicken, rubbing it in to coat. Season all over with the black pepper. To prevent them from scorching in the oven, tuck the chicken wing tips underneath the top of the breast.

Remove the preheated skillet from the oven and place it on a heat-safe surface, like your stovetop. Place the chicken breast-side up in the skillet (it should make very satisfying sizzles). Return the skillet to the oven and roast until the chicken skin starts to turn golden, about 15 minutes.

Remove the skillet from the oven and use tongs to turn the chicken over so it's breast-side down. Return to the oven and roast until the second side starts to turn golden, about 15 minutes.

Remove the skillet from the oven and turn the chicken breast-side up again. Return to the oven and roast until cooked through, another 15 minutes or so. The chicken is done when the juices run clear when pierced with a knife and an instant read thermometer in the thickest part of the thigh reads at least 160°F.

Transfer the chicken to a cutting board and let cool for at least 15 minutes before carving. Carve the chicken. Serve with the pan drippings spooned over the meat, rice, and veg.

ICED VEGETABLE SOMEN

Serves 4

On a hot summer night when the thought of eating anything warm makes me sweat, I make this. Somen is a Japanese noodle dish (as well as the name for the thin wheat noodles used in the dish) that's typically served chilled—don't skip the ice cubes. Adorn your bowl with any crunchy vegetables you have on hand.

1 (9.5-ounce) package somen noodles

2 cups mentsuyu (see Note)

Ice cubes, for serving

4 red radishes or Hakurei turnips, thinly sliced

2 Persian (mini) cucumbers, julienned

1 large carrot, peeled and julienned

4 scallions, thinly sliced

1 lemon or lime, very thinly sliced and seeded

Fresh ginger, for serving

Cook the noodles according to the package directions. Drain in a sieve and rinse with cold water. Set aside.

Set out four serving bowls. Divide the cooked noodles among the bowls, then pour ½ cup diluted mentsuyu into each. Add 2 or 3 ice cubes to each bowl. Arrange sliced radish, cucumber, and carrot over each bowl.

Just before serving, top each bowl with scallions and a few slices of lemon. Use a Microplane to grate a bit of ginger over each bowl and serve immediately.

NOTE: Mentsuyu is a flavorful Japanese soup base often accompanied by noodles. There are different brands of mentsuyu, some are concentrated (and there are various dilutions), while others are ready to use. If your mentsuyu is concentrated, combine the package's recommended amount of concentrate and water to reach 2 cups to make this recipe.

SWEET POTATO AND LAMB MEATBALLS

Serves 4 to 6

These baked meatballs are a flavor-packed crowd-pleaser, made with both lamb and beef along with sweet potato, chopped nuts, and fresh green herbs. I shape them into little footballs because they're much easier to form than perfect spheres. Try serving warm over rice or arugula and with torn fresh mint leaves or a drizzle of 1-2-3 Yogurt Sauce (page 64) on top.

½ cup Your Own Bread Crumbs (page 67) or store-bought

1 teaspoon granulated garlic, or ½ teaspoon garlic powder

¾ cup whole milk

1 egg

2 medium sweet potatoes, scrubbed and grated on the large holes of a box grater (about 1½ cups)

1 small red or yellow onion, grated on the large holes of a box grater

¼ cup finely chopped fresh parsley

¼ cup finely chopped walnuts

2 teaspoons ground cumin

1½ teaspoons sea salt

1 pound ground lamb

½ pound ground beef (80/20)

Preheat the oven to 425°F. Line two sheet pans with parchment paper.

In a large bowl, combine the bread crumbs and granulated garlic. Stir in the milk and set aside for 10 minutes to let the liquid absorb.

Use a fork to beat the egg into the rested milk/bread crumb mixture. Use the fork or your hands to mix in the sweet potatoes, onion, parsley, walnuts, cumin, and salt. Use your hands to gently incorporate the lamb and beef.

Pick up small handfuls of the mixture and gently roll between your palms to form about 2-inch football-shaped meatballs (you'll get 35 to 40). Spread out on the sheet pans.

Bake until the meat registers at least 165°F on an instant-read thermometer, 14 to 16 minutes, using tongs to flip the meatballs, switching racks halfway through.

SERVE WITH

1-2-3 Sauce (page 64)

Quick-Fermented Green Hot Sauce (page 60)

Leftover meatballs and 1-2-3 Sauce make a very good sandwich for lunch: Add Classic Dill Pickles (page 56) and/or Purple Cabbage Curtido (page 57) if you have them.

SHEET PAN KABOCHA-GINGER SOUP

Makes about 2½ quarts; serves 4 to 6

A soup this good seems like it should take a lot of effort, but the beauty of this recipe is it's largely passive. By simply roasting kabocha squash and leeks on a sheet pan you create all the rich, caramelized flavor for the finished product. If you'd like, use an immersion blender to puree the soup (skins and all) until smooth.

Gluten-free, vegan (if using vegan stock)

3 medium leeks (1 to 1½ pounds), white and light-green parts only

1 small kabocha squash (2½ to 3 pounds), scrubbed

⅓ cup extra-virgin olive oil, plus more for serving

1½ teaspoons sea salt, plus more to taste

Freshly ground black pepper

1 cup dry white wine

4 cups preferred stock (see $0 Scrap Stock, page 34)

1 cup water

2-inch piece fresh ginger, peeled and coarsely chopped

Flaky sea salt, for serving

Preheat the oven to 425°F. Place a sheet pan in the oven to preheat.

Slice the leeks into 1-inch chunks and place in a large bowl of water or a salad spinner. Swish around to remove dirt from the leeks; repeat with fresh water as needed until the leeks are clean. Dry on kitchen towels.

Halve the squash (no need to peel). Scoop out and discard the seeds and pulp, then slice each half into 2-inch wedges.

Spread out the squash and leeks on a sheet pan (it will be full). Drizzle everything with the olive oil and season with the salt and lots of black pepper. Roast, tossing halfway through, until the squash is very tender and starting to brown, 25 to 30 minutes.

Remove the vegetables from the oven. Transfer the roasted vegetables to a large pot. Immediately pour the white wine over the hot sheet pan to deglaze and use a spatula to scrape up any stuck-on caramelized bits. Scrape the wine and caramelized bits into the pot. Stir in the stock, water, and ginger.

Bring the mixture to a boil over high heat. Reduce the heat to medium, cover, and simmer, stirring occasionally, until the squash is so tender it nearly falls apart, about 10 minutes.

Turn off the heat. Use a wooden spoon to break up any large pieces of squash. Season with more salt and pepper to taste.

Ladle the soup into bowls. Drizzle each bowl with a splash of olive oil and a pinch of flaky sea salt.

NOTE: Kabocha is a Japanese winter squash that's usually sold alongside butternut and acorn varieties. It's a great choice for this method because the skin is delicate enough to be eaten once it's cooked. You can also use this recipe with other squash, but make sure to peel off the tough skin before blending.

SERVE WITH

Broth-Simmered Farro (page 48)

Easiest Rice (page 44)

Grilled Bread (page 107)

BROTHY CAVATELLI AND BEANS

Serves 4

Brothy pasta is near-instantaneous comfort food. This meal relies on a Component-Cooked basic, 60:40 Beans. I can quickly reheat the beans from my freezer by placing them in a covered pot over medium heat, stir in cooked pasta, and have a weeknight dinner that tastes like I spent all day cooking.

Vegan (if omitting anchovies)

¼ cup extra-virgin olive oil, plus more for drizzling

1 medium red or yellow onion, coarsely chopped

2 garlic cloves, thinly sliced

3 oil-packed anchovies (optional)

Sea salt and freshly ground black pepper

2 tablespoons tomato paste

3 cups cooked beans, such as 60:40 Beans (page 38), plus their cooking liquid or water

8 ounces cavatelli or preferred short pasta

5 ounces baby spinach or torn kale

Lemon wedges, for squeezing

In a large pot, heat the oil over medium heat. Add the onion, garlic, and anchovies (if using). Season with a pinch of salt and some black pepper and cook, stirring occasionally, until the vegetables are golden and the anchovies melt in, 5 to 8 minutes. Stir in the tomato paste and cook until it's starting to stick to the pot, another 1 to 2 minutes.

Stir in the beans and 2½ cups of their cooking liquid or water. Scrape up any stuck bits on the bottom of the pot. Let the mixture come to a simmer. Reduce the heat to low and continue to simmer.

While the bean mixture is simmering, bring a large pot of water to a boil over high heat. Stir in a handful of salt, then the pasta. Cook until just al dente according to the package directions, then use a spider strainer to scoop out the pasta and add to the bean mixture. Don't get rid of the pasta water yet.

Stir the spinach into the bean-and-pasta mixture, then season to taste with salt and pepper. If you'd like the mixture brothier, add reserved pasta water by the splash. Serve with lemon wedges for squeezing over. Best eaten immediately.

CRISPY-SKINNED SALMON OVER HERBED FARRO

Serves 4

Issey and I perfected this recipe many years ago when we were living in our Brooklyn apartment. Since then, everyone who tries it raves about one thing: the crispy skin. The key to making salmon skin you'll actually want to eat is to salt it liberally in advance. I prefer Atlantic salmon, which has pale pink-colored flesh and a buttery flavor. You don't need a nonstick pan for fish: Prevent any sticking by patting the skin dry before cooking, and ensuring your pan is properly heated before you add the fish.

4 center-cut, skin-on salmon fillets (see Note), 4 to 6 ounces each, scales removed

1½ teaspoons sea salt, plus more to taste

3 tablespoons apple cider vinegar or lemon juice

5 tablespoons extra-virgin olive oil

3 cups cooked grains, such as Broth-Simmered Farro (page 48)

1 cup tightly packed fresh tender herbs, such as parsley, cilantro, dill, basil, and/or mint leaves, finely chopped

6 ounces snap peas, coarsely chopped (about 1¼ cups)

4 scallions, thinly sliced

Freshly ground black pepper

Place the salmon skin-side up on a plate or small sheet pan. Sprinkle the skin of each fillet with ½ teaspoon salt. Refrigerate for at least 20 minutes (or up to 1 hour) while you make the farro salad.

In a large bowl, whisk together the vinegar and 3 tablespoons of the olive oil. Stir in the farro, herbs, snap peas, and scallions. Season with salt and pepper to taste.

Remove the salmon from the fridge and pat dry all over with paper towels, removing any excess salt from the skin. Season the skins with a few grinds of black pepper.

Heat a large carbon steel or stainless steel skillet over medium-high heat for 1 minute.

Add the remaining 2 tablespoons oil to the pan and swirl to coat. Nestle in the salmon, skin-side down, then reduce the heat to medium-low. Season each fillet with salt and pepper, then cover the pan (if you don't have a lid, use a sheet pan). Cook until the flesh is just opaque and flakes with a fork at the edges, and the skin easily lifts from the pan and is very crisp, 7 to 9 minutes. Use a fish spatula to remove the fish from the pan without tearing the skin. Place the fillets skin-side up on a plate.

Divide the farro among four bowls and top each with a piece of salmon, skin-side up.

NOTE: Look for 1- to 2-inch-wide fillets that are about 1 inch thick.

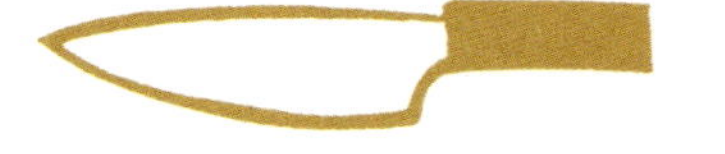

Component-Cooked Dinner Assemblies

Recipes from the Component Cooking chapter (page 32) can be reheated and combined to make an almost immediate dinner. Start with these ideas, and play around to see which other combinations sing to you.

Whole Poached Chicken (page 42) + The Perfect Sheet Pan Veg (page 62) + 1-2-3 Sauce (page 64)

Easiest Rice (page 44) + Soft-Boiled Eggs (page 43) + sliced cucumbers

Brine-Boiled Potatoes (page 51) + Sweet and Zingy Quick Pickles (page 58) + tinned mackerel or tuna + Grilled Bread (page 107)

Broth-Simmered Farro (page 48) + 60:40 Beans (page 38) + Nuts 'n' Herbs Sauce (page 65)

Whole-Poached Chicken (page 42, shredded, with poaching liquid) + Broth-Simmered Farro (page 48) + chopped Gingered Carrots (page 54)

Baked Whole Sweet Potatoes (page 61) + Purple Cabbage Curtido (page 57) + 1-2-3 Sauce (page 64)

60:40 Beans (page 38) + Soft-Boiled Eggs (page 43) + Sweet and Zingy Quick Pickles (page 58) or tender greens

$0 Scrap Stock (page 34) + Baked Whole Sweet Potatoes (page 61) + Broth-Simmered Farro (page 48)

ON

WEEKENDS

Weekends, to me, are synonymous with meals that offer an invitation to gather and enjoy. With a bit of extra time on hand, I like to let a special meal be a weekend activity to look forward to. Sunday mornings in my home always start with pancakes and a steaming pot of coffee. "Pancake Sunday" is the small ritual that we enjoy as a family, but it's also a sweet way to send off overnight guests who are visiting our upstate home from the city.

These slow days are the perfect setting for an early evening meal. I like to make a slow-cooked braise, grill veg from my farmers' market haul, or stew a pot of beans earlier in the day, which leaves time for everyone to return for seconds later. While some of these recipes take a little longer than the weekday recipes, they're all infused with a hands-off ease that makes them highly achievable.

MAPLE-CINNAMON COFFEE

Each recipe serves 2 to 4

On weekends, I like to brew freshly ground coffee with a bit of cinnamon. Its aroma fills the whole house with warmth. I have a hot pour-over and an iced cold brew method, which I rotate through with the seasons. Maple syrup is the perfect coffee sweetener because it's low glycemic, so it won't spike your blood sugar first thing in the morning.

POUR-OVER METHOD

600 grams (2½ cups) filtered water

35 grams (about 3 tablespoons) medium-fine ground coffee beans (see Note)

¼ teaspoon ground cinnamon

1 tablespoon maple syrup, plus more to taste

Milk, as desired

Place the water in an electric water heater or kettle over medium-high heat and bring to a low boil. Set up a coffee filter inside a filter dripper placed over a heatproof carafe or Chemex.

Using a circular motion, add a 2-second pour of water over the filter to just moisten it—no water should drip into the carafe.

Add the ground coffee and cinnamon to the filter. Using the circular motion, slowly pour in just enough water to cover the coffee, then wait 30 seconds to let the flavors bloom in the warmth. Continue to slowly pour, letting the coffee drip into the carafe until you've used all the water. The brewing process should take 6 to 8 minutes.

Remove the filter and stir the syrup into the coffee. Pour into cups with milk as desired and more syrup to taste.

NOTE: For medium-fine ground coffee for a pour-over, grind beans to the texture of sand.

COLD BREW METHOD

80 grams (1 cup) coarsely ground coffee beans (see Note)

1 teaspoon ground cinnamon

1.2 kilograms (5 cups) filtered water

2 tablespoons maple syrup, plus more to taste

Ice, as desired

Milk, as desired

In one 2-quart or two 1-quart mason jar(s) or a large bowl, stir together the coffee and cinnamon. Stir in the water, making sure all the grounds are moistened. Cover, transfer to the refrigerator, and chill overnight (or up to 24 hours).

Set up a fine-mesh sieve lined with a piece of cheesecloth or a coffee filter over another large jar, carafe, or medium bowl. Pour the steeped coffee through to strain. Stir in the maple syrup.

Pour into ice-filled glasses with milk as desired and more syrup to taste.

NOTE: For coarsely ground coffee for cold brew, grind beans to the texture of coarse salt.

CREPE-Y WHOLE WHEAT PANCAKES WITH LEMON BERRY SYRUP

Makes 10 to 12 pancakes

These crepe-style pancakes are inspired by the Polish-style pancakes Issey grew up eating with his father's side of the family. The best way to enjoy them is to pour syrup down the center, and then roll it up like a crepe and slice. These pancakes cook very quickly, which is great if you don't like waiting.

1⅔ cups (400g) whole milk

3 large eggs

¼ cup plus 2 teaspoons (70g) water

1 cup (125g) whole wheat flour

1 cup (125g) all-purpose flour

1 teaspoon sea salt

1 teaspoon salted butter

Maple syrup, Lemon Berry Syrup (recipe follows), or Skillet Jam (page 68), for serving

In a large bowl, whisk together the milk, eggs, and water until smooth. Whisk in both flours and the salt, continuing to whisk to form a loose, smooth batter. Set the batter aside and let rest for 10 minutes.

Heat a medium carbon steel pan over medium heat for 2 minutes. Add the butter to the hot pan and use a paper towel to rub it around the surface. Hang onto the towel, as you'll use this to regrease the pan.

Use a measuring cup or ladle to pour about ⅓ cup of batter into the pan. Use the bottom of the ladle (or a spoon), applying very light pressure, to spread out the batter in a spiral motion from the center out, into a paper-thin pancake, making sure not to tear through the bottom as it starts to set. Continue to cook until the top looks matte, about 30 seconds. Gently guide a spatula under the pancake and quickly flip. (Once flipped, the surface should look lightly golden brown.) I like to use a fish spatula for flipping because it is super-thin and flexible. Cook on the second side until air bubbles start to form underneath the pancake, another 20 to 30 seconds.

Transfer the pancake to a large plate (the second side should be golden brown with spots of darker gold) and cover with a towel to keep it warm while you cook the rest of the pancakes. Wipe the surface of the pan with the buttered towel and repeat to cook each remaining pancake.

Serve the pancakes warm with syrup or jam.

LEMON BERRY SYRUP

Makes a scant ½ cup

⅓ cup maple syrup

2 tablespoons Skillet Jam (page 68) or preferred store-bought

1 teaspoon fresh lemon juice, plus more to taste

Pinch of sea salt

I find that cooking fruit inside of pancakes doesn't deliver a great flavor or texture to the pancake—it also doesn't do the fruit any favors. Try adding a bit of jam to your syrup instead. This will work well with any jam or simple stewed fruit (I like cherries or apricots), or even an apple butter.

In a small bowl, whisk together the syrup, jam, juice, and salt until smooth.

COOK TOGETHER

You may live in a bustling family home like mine, or you may enjoy more peaceful solitude in your daily rhythm. It's easy for a household to fall into a habit of letting one person handle all of the kitchen tasks. Whatever your circumstance, find a way to cook with others. This can be in preparation for a big holiday meal or as simple as inviting a friend over on a Sunday night to make something you both like. Invite your spouse, roommate, or dinner guests into the kitchen to act as sous-chefs. Children are great helpers in the kitchen, too: Cutting out cookies, mixing pancake batter, sprinkling seasonings, and sorting through produce are all nice activities to welcome them into. My older daughter, Ruby, perches over our countertop while standing on a dining chair as she helps. When cooking is communal, it's not a chore to be endured, but a group experience to be enjoyed.

CLASSIC CURRANT SCONES

Makes 8 scones

I prefer to make these with whole wheat flour, which gives them a bit more texture and provides a nutty contrast to the sweet currants. When I was testing this recipe, I made a batch for my neighbor who had just welcomed a new baby. When her English father came by to drop off the plate with compliments, I knew we had nailed this one. Serve with soft salted butter and Skillet Jam (page 68).

2½ cups (310g) whole wheat flour, plus more for dusting

⅓ cup (50g) dried currants

2 tablespoons cane sugar, plus more for sprinkling

2 teaspoons baking powder

½ teaspoon ground cinnamon (optional)

¼ teaspoon baking soda

¼ teaspoon sea salt

8 tablespoons (113g/1 stick) cold unsalted butter, cut into ½-inch pieces

1 egg, lightly beaten

¾ cup plus 2 tablespoons (209g) soured milk (see Note)

Preheat the oven to 350°F. Line a sheet pan with parchment paper.

In a large bowl, use a fork or your fingers to combine the flour, currants, sugar, baking powder, cinnamon (if using), baking soda, and salt.

Toss the butter cubes into the flour mixture to coat. Use your fingers to pinch and smash the butter into small flakes (the largest should be about ¼ inch wide), gently working the butter into the flour mixture as you pinch.

Use a fork to mix the egg into the soured milk. Set aside 1 tablespoon of this mixture in a small bowl.

Make a well in the center of the flour/butter mixture, then pour in the egg/sour milk mixture. Use the fork to gently mix together until it forms a shaggy dough. Use your hands to knead the mixture once or twice to make sure there are no areas of dry flour, but don't overwork it into a solid mass.

Lightly dust a work surface with a bit of flour, then pour out the dough. Gently pat the dough into a 1-inch-thick mass, then fold it in half. Gently pat down the dough again into a disk about 8 inches wide and 1 inch thick.

Use a pastry brush to coat the surface of the disk with the reserved egg/sour milk mixture. Sprinkle with a bit of sugar. Use a floured knife or bench scraper to cut the disk into 8 wedges.

Bake the scones until slightly puffed and golden, 25 to 30 minutes. Let cool for 5 minutes on the sheet pan, then serve warm.

NOTE: To make soured milk, combine ¾ cup (175g) whole milk with 2 tablespoons apple cider vinegar. Let sit at room temperature for 5 minutes to curdle.

ISSEY'S PUFFY SOURDOUGH PANCAKES

Makes about 10 pancakes

These are pillowy, crisp-edged pancakes, made extra tender and fluffy with the addition of yogurt and beaten egg white. We make these with leftovers from feeding our sourdough starter, also known as discard, which cuts back on waste and also makes the pancakes a little easier to digest than those made with just white flour. (See the following page for more on sourdough starter.)

1⅔ cups (200g) all-purpose flour

1 teaspoon baking soda

1 teaspoon baking powder

¼ teaspoon sea salt

2 large eggs, separated

240 grams (1 heaping cup) sourdough starter discard (see Note)

¾ cup plus 2 tablespoons (200g) whole-milk Greek yogurt

¼ cup (60g) whole milk or water

2 tablespoons cane sugar

4 tablespoons (60g) unsalted butter, melted

Extra-virgin olive oil, for frying

Butter, unsalted or salted, for serving

Maple syrup or Lemon Berry Syrup (page 157), for serving

In a small bowl, whisk together the flour, baking soda, baking powder, and salt. Set aside.

Place the egg whites in a medium bowl. Use a whisk to beat until they form stiff peaks (if you hold the whisk upright, the beaten white should hold its pointy tip). Set aside.

In a large bowl, whisk together the sourdough discard, yogurt, milk, sugar, and egg yolks until they are well combined.

Whisk the flour mixture into the sourdough discard mixture until just combined. Using a folding motion, gently mix in the melted butter, then gently fold in the beaten egg whites until just combined.

In a 12-inch cast-iron skillet (see Notes), heat 2 tablespoons oil over medium heat. When the oil ripples, use a measuring cup or ladle to spoon about ⅓ cup of batter into the pan. Immediately use the bottom of the ladle (or a spoon) to spread out the batter about 4 inches wide. Repeat with a second scoop of batter.

Let the pancakes cook on the first side until they start to form small bubbles around the edges and center, and the surface starts to look matte, 3 to 4 minutes. Flip the pancakes. Cook until golden brown on the bottom, 2 to 3 minutes. Re-oil the pan and repeat until you've used all the batter. If the pancakes start to get really dark on the first side before they're set, lower the heat slightly.

Transfer the pancakes to a plate and serve immediately. Alternatively, to keep them warm and crisp while cooking the rest, place the cooked pancakes on a sheet pan in a 200°F oven.

Serve the pancakes warm with butter and syrup.

NOTE: If you don't have sourdough discard, stir together 120 grams (about ½ cup) of water and 120 grams (a scant 1 cup) of all-purpose flour in a large bowl; if you know the night before that you want to make pancakes, lightly cover and leave this mixture out at room temperature overnight to aerate, then follow the recipe as written.

ON KEEPING A SOURDOUGH STARTER

Even if you don't bake your own bread, it's worth keeping a sourdough starter. Starter is a mixture of flour and water that's fermented with wild yeast and bacteria in the air, and can be used in place of packaged yeast. The little microbes that live in a starter help to make bread easier to digest than loaves made with commercial yeast. Starter can be added to cookies, crackers, and other flour-based recipes for a sour tang and healthy prebiotics.

You can make your own sourdough starter with flour, water, and time (it takes a few weeks), but a great way to get going immediately is to ask for some from your favorite bread bakery—all you need is a few grams. Starters need to be "fed" regularly with fresh flour and water. Like tending to small plants, it's a nice exercise in slowing down to care for something. The first time you get some sourdough starter, measure out how much you have into a clean glass jar (using a digital scale and grams is easiest). I like to start with 20 grams of starter. From there, mix in equal parts (try 100 grams each) of all-purpose flour and water. Lightly lay on the jar lid and let it sit out on the counter for at least 12 or up to 24 hours. The starter will bubble up and aerate as it sits. It should be fed every 24 hours, or stored in the fridge and fed once a week. Every time you need to feed your starter, start by pouring 20 grams of the starter into a clean jar, then mix in 100 grams each of fresh flour and water to the new jar with 20 grams starter. Any leftover starter from the first jar, known as "discard," can be composted; but it's also perfectly edible. We like to add it to pancakes (see page 161).

SOUR DOUG

GRILL THE GARDEN

I like to turn the classic grilling lineup of burgers and hot dogs on its head, highlighting the glut of vegetables at their absolute peak in summertime. Grilled fresh corn, zucchini, and peppers are gorgeously rich in color and texture, and feed a larger group for a better cost than meat alone.

Grilling brings out vegetables' natural sweetness, and the layer of char creates savory depth. You can grill any vegetable you love (fruit like peaches, plums, and pineapple benefit from a little char, too). I like to throw a mix of vegetables on the grill—whatever looks good that week—and eat as is, or add some simple dressings. Leftover grilled veg stores well in the fridge and is delicious reheated and served over a dish of creamy polenta or cooked rice.

How to Grill

Prepare your grill for high heat, which will give you a nice char on the outside of the vegetables while still maintaining textural integrity. It can be helpful to set up the grill for both direct heat (directly over the flame) and indirect heat (slightly aside from the flame). Think of direct heat like a stovetop and indirect like the oven.

Slice your veg into large chunks so they don't fall through the grates. Place on a sheet pan, drizzle with olive oil, and season liberally with salt.

Everything will take a different amount of time to cook—pull things off the grill when they've started to wilt and are charred but not burnt. If grilling whole eggplant or potatoes, use indirect heat to allow them to cook through. When they're fork-tender, switch to direct heat to finish with some char. Remove grilled veg back to the sheet pan, then serve as is, or dress up a bit (see Grilled Assemblies on page 166).

What to Grill

Cabbage and radicchio

Cut into 2-inch wedges, leaving the core in to hold the leaves together.

Summer squash

Halve, quarter, or slice into thick rounds.

Sweet peppers

Grill them halved until charred. For a riff on roasted red peppers, grill whole over direct heat until the skin is black. Transfer to a bowl with a lid over the top for 10 minutes to steam. Scrape the charred skin off with a knife, then use your fingers to pull off the stem (most of the seeds will come out with it). Scrape off any remaining seeds.

Green beans and asparagus

Trim off the stem ends from the green beans and the woody ends of the asparagus. Add perpendicular to the grates so they don't fall through, or heat a cast-iron skillet on the grill and cook them right in the pan.

CONTINUED

Eggplant

Look for long, slender Japanese eggplants or tiny varieties like Fairy Tale (the flesh is sweeter and they have fewer seeds than other varieties).

Potatoes and sweet potatoes

Whole (poked a few times with a knife and wrapped in foil) or halved

Cauliflower and broccoli

Slice into thick planks (or cut into florets and place on a cast-iron skillet to avoid anything falling through the grates).

Corn

Pull back the husks, leaving the stalk on, and grill whole.

Citrus, too

Lemons, limes, and oranges can be halved and grilled. Drizzle the smoky juices over everything on your plate.

Don't forget bread

Drizzle thick slices of crusty sourdough bread generously with oil, then grill on both sides until charred.

Grilled Assemblies

I think there are few greater summer joys than a plate full of freshly grilled veg. Squeeze the juice of a grilled lemon over the top, and top with a little flaky sea salt to complete the picture. But a little assembly can turn your components into a beautiful finished dish, too:

Zucchini and corn (kernels cut off cobs) + lemon or lime + fresh mint

Radicchio and sweet peppers + toasted walnuts + balsamic

Japanese eggplant + maple syrup + 1-2-3 Tahini Sauce (page 64)

Scallions and white potatoes + rice vinegar + fresh cilantro

Green beans + miso mixed with rice vinegar + sesame seeds

Whole corn + butter + lime + grated Parmesan

Red or green cabbage + 1-2-3 Yogurt Sauce (page 64)

Broccoli or cauliflower + toasted sesame oil + Quick-Fermented Green Hot Sauce (page 60)

GROW SOMETHING, ANYTHING!

Whether you have a windowsill or a large plot, you can grow something. Don't let your notion of green thumbs and who has them sway you from the possibilities. When you choose to grow an herb or a tomato plant, or even a tray of wheatgrass, you connect yourself to the life process that creates all of our food. You don't need to tend a prolific vegetable patch to begin to see the connection between the way a plant is nurtured and how it feeds us. This is not an exercise in self-sufficiency but instead a kind reminder of our own interconnectedness with nature itself.

If you want an easy way to get started, oregano is one of the most amenable herbs to windowsill gardening. As a Mediterranean plant, it thrives on a lack of water, and it only grows back stronger when plucked. A few leaves of fresh oregano add a peppery bite to salads and pastas that's entirely different from the dried herb. If you harvest more than you can eat at once, set it out to dry in a warm, sunny spot and enjoy your own homegrown addition to the spice cabinet.

The gardener learns nothing when his carrots thrive, unless the success is hard won against a background of prior disappointment. Outright success is dumb, disaster frequently eloquent.

—*Michael Pollan,* Second Nature

SEASONAL BAKED PASTA

Serves 6

This baked pasta carries us through the year, swapping in different seasonal ingredients to highlight what's delicious at the current moment. You can make this to serve a larger group, or to serve a smaller group with leftovers (I think it's even better when reheated).

Your choice of seasonal ingredients (see opposite)

Sea salt

1 pound short pasta, such as rigatoni, cavatappi, farfalle, or ziti

½ cup bread crumbs, homemade (page 67) or store-bought panko

1 tablespoon olive oil

Freshly ground black pepper

1 cup whole-milk ricotta cheese

½ cup finely grated pecorino or Parmesan cheese

2 garlic cloves, finely chopped

2 teaspoons grated lemon zest (from about ½ lemon)

2 tablespoons fresh lemon juice (from about ½ lemon)

Preheat the oven to 425°F with a rack in the lower third.

In a large, ovenproof pot such as a Dutch oven, cook the seasonal ingredients as directed. Turn off the heat.

Bring another large pot of water to a boil over high heat. Add a handful of salt, then stir in the pasta. Cook the pasta for 2 minutes less than al dente according to the package directions. Reserving 1 cup of the pasta cooking water, drain the pasta into a colander.

In a small bowl, toss together the bread crumbs and olive oil with a pinch of salt and pepper.

Add the drained pasta to the Dutch oven with the seasonal ingredients. Stir in the ricotta, pecorino, garlic, lemon zest, lemon juice, and ½ cup of the reserved pasta cooking water. If the mixture seems dry, add more pasta water by the splash. Season with more salt and pepper to taste.

Sprinkle the bread crumb mixture over everything. Place the pot in the oven and bake until the bread crumbs are golden brown, 15 to 20 minutes. For more color, broil on high for 1 to 3 minutes.

Let cool slightly, then serve.

Spring

ASPARAGUS AND PEAS

Use **1 pound asparagus**, trimmed and sliced ½ inch thick; and **½ pound (about 1 cup) shelled fresh peas**. Sauté the asparagus in **⅓ cup oil** with **a pinch of salt and freshly ground pepper**, stirring often, until just tender, 3 to 5 minutes. To cook the peas, add them to the pasta water 3 minutes before draining, then drain with the pasta.

Fall

WINTER SQUASH AND LEEK

Heat **⅓ cup extra-virgin olive oil** and add **1 pound winter squash** (butternut, acorn, honeynut, etc.), cut into ½-inch chunks; and **½ pound leeks**, trimmed, washed, and coarsely chopped. Sauté together over medium heat with **a pinch of salt and freshly ground pepper**, stirring often, until the vegetables are tender and starting to char in spots, 10 to 15 minutes.

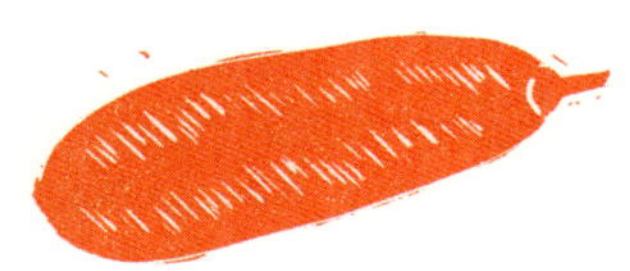

Summer

ZUCCHINI AND SWEET PEPPERS

Heat **⅓ cup extra-virgin olive oil** and add **1 pound zucchini or summer squash**, halved and thinly sliced; and **½ pound bell peppers**, thinly sliced. Sauté together over medium heat with **a pinch of salt and freshly ground pepper**, stirring often, until the vegetables are tender and starting to char in spots, 8 to 10 minutes.

Winter

BROCCOLI RABE AND ITALIAN SAUSAGE

Use **1 pound broccoli rabe or kale** (including stems and ribs), coarsely chopped; and **½ pound sweet or hot Italian sausage**, casings removed. Heat **¼ cup extra-virgin olive oil** in the pot over medium-high, then add the sausage to the pan in 2-inch chunks. Let cook, tossing every few minutes, until browned all over. Break up the sausage with a spoon into bite-size pieces and continue to cook until no longer pink, another 3 minutes or so, then remove to a plate, leaving the rendered fat in the pan. Reduce the heat to medium. Sauté the greens until just tender, 3 to 5 minutes, season with **a pinch of salt and freshly ground pepper**, then return the sausage to the pan.

FENNEL, CORN, AND CLAM CHOWDER

Serves 6

Chowder is my favorite use for corn cobs left over from a season of summer eating. This uses my recipe for sweet corn cob stock, but you can use any stock you have on hand. If you don't have clams, this soup is just as delicious with a mix of extra vegetables like chopped zucchini or carrots, or shelled peas tossed in at the end.

4 cups Corn Cob Stock (page 37) or stock of choice

8 tablespoons (4 ounces/1 stick) unsalted butter, cut into pieces

4 small leeks, white and light-green parts only, coarsely chopped

1 large fennel bulb, coarsely chopped, any fronds reserved

2 celery stalks, sliced ½-inch thick

Sea salt and freshly ground black pepper

3 tablespoons all-purpose flour

2 cups whole milk

2 large Yukon Gold potatoes, cut into ½-inch chunks

1½ cups fresh corn kernels (from about 2 ears)

Two 6.5-ounce cans chopped or whole clams (see Notes)

1 cup chopped fresh dill or parsley, for serving

In a medium pot, warm the stock over medium-low heat until steaming.

Meanwhile, in a heavy-bottomed pot, such as a Dutch oven, melt half of the butter over medium heat. Add the leeks, fennel, celery, a big pinch of salt, and some pepper. Cook, stirring occasionally, until the vegetables are softened and just starting to brown, 5 to 8 minutes. Remove to a bowl and set aside.

Add the flour to the pot. Stirring constantly, let the flour toast until it smells nutty, about 2 minutes. Stir in the remaining butter. Continue to cook, stirring, until the mixture is smooth, bubbling, and lightly golden, about 1 minute.

Stirring constantly, pour 1 cup of the warm stock into the flour mixture until smooth. Slowly stir in the remaining stock and the milk until the mixture is smooth.

Stir in the potatoes and the reserved leeks, fennel, and celery. Let the mixture come to a simmer. Reduce the heat to medium-low and cook, stirring occasionally until the potatoes are fork-tender, 10 to 15 minutes.

Reduce the heat to low and stir in the corn and the clams and their juices. Season with more salt and pepper to taste. Let cook until the clams and corn are warmed through, about 5 minutes. Turn off the heat.

Serve with fresh dill and reserved fennel fronds.

NOTE: To swap in fresh clams, scrub 15 to 20 small clams, such as littleneck, then soak in a large bowl of cold water with a handful of salt for 15 minutes; drain and repeat twice, ensuring all the grit comes out of the clams. Add to the soup halfway through simmering—they're cooked through when the shells open (discard any that don't open after 25 minutes).

SWEET AND SPICY BLACK-EYED PEAS

Serves 6

I grew up eating black-eyed peas every week, usually with a side of slow-cooked, buttery cabbage. This recipe is true to my grandmother's preparation, but with lots of chopped aromatic veg to up the sweetness.

Gluten-free, vegan

---

1 pound dried black-eyed peas (about 2 cups)

One 3-inch piece kombu, lightly crushed into pieces (optional; see Note, page 38)

½ cup extra-virgin olive oil, plus more for drizzling

2 teaspoons cumin seeds

2 teaspoons fennel seeds

2 medium red bell peppers, finely chopped

2 medium yellow, red, or sweet white onions, finely chopped

2 celery stalks, finely chopped

1 large carrot, scrubbed and finely chopped

Sea salt and freshly ground black pepper

3 tablespoons tomato paste

2 tablespoons smoked paprika, hot or sweet

1 teaspoon red pepper flakes

1 tablespoon cane sugar

2 tablespoons apple cider vinegar

Rinse the dried peas thoroughly in a colander.

Transfer to a large bowl along with the kombu. Pour water into the bowl until the peas are covered by 3 inches. Let them soak for at least 6 or up to 12 hours.

Drain the peas and rinse.

In a large heavy-bottomed pot, heat the oil over medium heat. Add the cumin and fennel seeds and cook until fragrant, about 1 minute.

Stir in the vegetables, a big pinch of salt, and lots of black pepper. Cover and cook until they're softened but not browned, 6 to 8 minutes.

Uncover the pot and continue to cook, stirring occasionally, until the vegetables start to brown, another 15 to 20 minutes.

Stir in the tomato paste, smoked paprika, and pepper flakes. Cook, stirring, until the mixture gets thick and sticky, 2 to 3 minutes. Add the peas, sugar, 2 teaspoons salt, and enough water to cover everything by 2 inches. Bring the mixture to a boil.

Cover the pot partially with a lid, reduce the heat to medium-low, and cook, stirring very occasionally, until the beans are tender and the liquid has reduced a bit, 1 to 2 hours. Stir in the vinegar, season with more salt to taste, and let cook for another 10 minutes to let the flavors meld.

Ladle into bowls and top with a drizzle of olive oil.

SERVE WITH

Easiest Rice (page 44)

Sweet Rosemary Cornbread (page 213)

FALL-APART BRAISED BEEF SHANKS

Serves 6

I love cooking with tough, bone-in cuts of beef, as it's a mostly passive process where you'll let the beef do its thing in the oven for a couple of hours. Cooking low and slow breaks down tougher cuts of meat until they're fall-off-the-bone tender. As the meat slowly braises in liquid, you'll also make an incredibly rich broth that's filled with healthy minerals and collagen. I recommend spooning liberally over one of the options listed below.

Gluten-free

---

4 pounds bone-in beef shanks

Sea salt

3 tablespoons extra-virgin olive oil

6 garlic cloves, smashed and peeled

2 medium yellow onions, coarsely chopped

2 tablespoons freshly ground coriander

1 cup dry red wine

3 cups preferred stock (see $0 Scrap Stock, page 34)

1 pound carrots, scrubbed and coarsely chopped

1 tablespoon apple cider vinegar, plus more to taste

Preheat the oven to 275°F with a rack in the lower third.

Season the beef shanks all over with 2 teaspoons salt.

In a large Dutch oven (at least 6 quarts), heat 1 tablespoon of the oil over medium-high heat until rippling. Working in batches to avoid crowding the pot, sear the shanks until deeply golden, 4 to 6 minutes per side. Transfer the seared shanks to a sheet pan or large plate.

Add the remaining 2 tablespoons oil to the pot along with the garlic, onions, and a big pinch of salt. Scrape up any bits stuck to the pot and cook, stirring occasionally, until starting to soften, another 4 to 5 minutes.

Stir in the coriander and let sizzle for 30 seconds, then add the wine. Let the liquid simmer until slightly reduced, another 4 to 6 minutes.

Pour in the stock and stir to combine. Nestle in the seared shanks and the carrots, ensuring the meat is mostly submerged (it's okay if some vegetables are poking up through the liquid, they'll sink in as everything cooks). Sprinkle with another big pinch of salt. Cover the pot and transfer to the oven.

Let the shanks slowly braise until they are fall-apart tender (use a fork to pull at the meat, it should easily shred), 3 to 4 hours. Start checking every 30 minutes after 3 hours—the timing ultimately depends on how thick your shanks are.

Remove from the oven. Use a slotted spoon to remove the meat from the pot to a serving platter. Stir the vinegar into the braising liquid. Taste the liquid and season with more vinegar and salt before serving.

NOTE: To stretch it across even more servings, shred the meat right in the pot, then return to the stove over medium heat (uncovered) and let the liquid reduce by about one-third into a hearty sauce to toss with cooked pasta.

SERVE WITH

Cooked pasta

Polenta (see method on page 134)

Braised Collards with Smoky Shiitake (page 181)

Brine-Boiled Potatoes (page 51)

Easiest Rice (page 44)

STEAMING MISO NABE

Serves 6

Nabe refers to a Japanese style of hot pot: Batches of meat and vegetables are cooked in a simmering broth, then served out of the clay pot (donabe, see page 47)) right at the table. This miso nabe works more like a classic stew and is cooked on the stovetop. It's great for feeding a group, so I love it for entertaining, but it's simple enough to be a weeknight family staple.

You can use different miso pastes to add a subtle variety in flavor to your nabe broth. White miso is mild and sweet, whereas red miso has a sharper, saltier flavor. Kyushu, the Japanese island where most of my husband's family lives, is known for mugi miso, which is made with barley and has notes of caramel.

Vegan option

---

5 medium Yukon Gold potatoes, scrubbed and peeled

3 medium carrots, scrubbed and peeled

½ pound skinless pork belly or one 16-ounce package extra-firm tofu

4 cups preferred stock (see $0 Scrap Stock, page 34)

1½ cups water

¼ cup soy sauce

¼ cup red miso

1 pound napa cabbage, cored and cut into 2-inch chunks

8 ounces shiitake mushrooms, stems trimmed, and caps sliced ¼ inch thick (about 3 cups)

2-inch piece fresh ginger, peeled and very thinly sliced

1 bunch scallions (6 to 8), thinly sliced on the bias, for serving

Cut the potatoes lengthwise into quarters. Use a sharp paring knife or vegetable peeler to round off the sharp angles from the cut pieces of potato (see opposite), then set aside. Cut the carrots into 1-inch chunks. Round the edges of the carrots and set aside with the potatoes.

Slice the pork belly into long strips 1 inch wide, then slice crosswise ¼ inch thick. (If using tofu, cut into 1-inch cubes.)

In a 2½- to 3-quart donabe or large heavy-bottomed pot, such as a Dutch oven, combine the stock, water, and soy sauce. Dollop the miso in small spoonfuls into the liquid, then use a chopstick or whisk to evenly blend in the miso.

Arrange the potatoes, carrots, cabbage, mushrooms, pork belly, and ginger in sections of the pot (it's okay if there's some overlap). Set over medium heat, cover the pot, and cook until the broth is simmering, the pork is just about cooked through, and the carrots and potatoes are just fork-tender, 20 to 30 minutes.

Uncover and stir the mixture. Cover, reduce the heat to low, and cook until the vegetables are cooked through (a paring knife should easily slide through the carrots and potatoes), 10 to 15 minutes.

Ladle into serving bowls and top generously with scallions.

SERVE WITH

Easiest Rice (page 44)

HOW TO MENTORI CUT VEGETABLES FOR STEWS

This recipe uses the Japanese technique of *mentori* to prep the vegetables for stewing. Rounding corners of the raw pieces of produce with a sharp knife (or vegetable peeler) prevents the edges from breaking off during cooking. This also increases the surface area of the vegetable, allowing it to better absorb the broth, and rendering more flavorful veg.

BRAISED COLLARDS WITH SMOKY SHIITAKE

Serves 6

Sweet, smoky collard greens, stewed with ham hocks, are a soul food staple I grew up eating. One year, we needed to figure out how to re-create the dish for my in-laws, who don't eat meat. Issey came up with the brilliant trick of cooking shiitake mushrooms until they looked like "bacon bits"—the smoky, savory flavor worked perfectly. Now, this is our preferred method for making collard greens every winter.

Gluten-free, vegan

⅓ cup plus 2 tablespoons extra-virgin olive oil

8 ounces shiitake mushrooms, stems removed, caps diced

2 teaspoons freshly ground coriander

2 teaspoons ground cumin

Sea salt

1 green bell pepper, diced

1 medium red or yellow onion, diced

1 medium carrot, scrubbed and diced

2 teaspoons sweet paprika

1 bunch collard greens (about 12 ounces), thinly sliced, including stems and midribs

1½ cups preferred stock (see $0 Scrap Stock, page 34)

¼ cup apple cider vinegar

2 teaspoons cane sugar

In a Dutch oven, heat ⅓ cup of the oil over medium heat until it shimmers. Stir in the mushrooms. They may soak up the oil at first and it will seem like there's not enough, but the mushrooms will slowly release the oil and excess liquid as they cook. Cook, stirring occasionally, until the mushrooms are starting to brown, about 6 minutes. Add the coriander and cumin. Continue to cook, stirring occasionally, until the mushrooms are browned, crisped, and shrunken significantly, 5 to 6 more minutes.

Turn off the heat. Use a slotted spoon to remove the mushrooms to a bowl, leaving the excess oil. Toss the mushrooms and a big pinch of salt and set aside.

Set the pan over medium-high heat and add the remaining 2 tablespoons oil, the bell pepper, onion, carrot, and 1 teaspoon salt. Cook, stirring occasionally, until the vegetables are softened and starting to brown, 8 to 10 minutes. Stir in the paprika.

Stir in the reserved cooked mushrooms, collards, stock, vinegar, and sugar. Partially cover the pot, reduce the heat to medium-low, and let cook until the collards are wilted and the liquid has reduced a bit, about 30 minutes, stirring halfway through. After this point, you can cover the pot, reduce the heat to low, and continue cooking for up to 2 hours if you have the time, and the collards will continue to soften. Season with more salt to taste and serve.

SERVE WITH

Easiest Rice (page 44)

Fall-Apart Braised Beef Shanks (page 177)

Sweet and Spicy Black-Eyed Peas (page 174)

Whole Poached Chicken (page 42)

WHOLE ROASTED SNAPPER WITH COUSCOUS AND MINT

Serves 6

I love the display of a whole roasted fish. It feels celebratory, but it's one of the more economical proteins, and a very speedy way to get a group meal on the table. This is a good opportunity to visit your local fishmonger (at a farmers' market or the fish counter of a grocery store) and ask for what's very fresh that day and good for whole roasting. Look for medium-size whole fish with clear, bright eyes and firm skin. Typically, whole fish will come scaled and gutted. Ask your fishmonger to do it if they haven't already.

2 lemons or limes

2 whole red snappers (3 pounds total), cleaned and scaled

Sea salt and freshly ground black pepper

2 tablespoons extra-virgin olive oil

COUSCOUS

2 cups couscous

Preferred stock (see $0 Scrap Stock, page 34)

Sea salt

1 bunch scallions (6 to 8), thinly sliced

Olive oil

Freshly ground pepper

1 cup fresh mint leaves, roughly torn, for garnish

Preheat the oven to 450°F. Line a sheet pan with parchment paper.

Thinly slice 1 lemon and remove any seeds.

Lay the fish on the sheet pan and pat dry. Cut 3 diagonal slashes on each side of the fish just to the bone. Season each fish (inside and out) with 1½ teaspoons sea salt and some pepper. Stuff each fish cavity with the sliced citrus. Drizzle the fish with 1 tablespoon of the oil, then flip over and drizzle with the remaining 1 tablespoon oil.

Roast the fish until the flesh is firm to the touch, opaque, and easily flakes with a fork, 15 to 20 minutes.

Meanwhile, cook the couscous: In a saucepan, cook the couscous according to the package directions with stock in place of water and a pinch of salt. Fluff the couscous and stir in the scallions, a splash of olive oil, and more salt and pepper to taste. When you're ready to serve, stir in the mint.

When the fish is cooked through, let it cool for 5 minutes, then remove it to a serving plate. Cut the remaining citrus into wedges for juicing. Carve the fish (see page 185) and serve with the couscous, drizzled with more olive oil. Best eaten immediately.

SERVE WITH

Any of the Chunky Salads (page 108)

HOW TO CARVE COOKED FISH

Whole fish like snapper can be quite bony, so it's best to carve before serving (and keep an eye out for any stray bones as you eat).

On the sheet pan, a cutting board, or a plate, position the fish horizontal to you. Using a spoon and a table knife, gently nudge out the fin bones from the top and bottom of the fish, scraping out any little bones that come with it. Discard the bones.

Guide the knife and spoon to separate the head from the top fillet, cutting through until you hit bone. Repeat with the tail side.

Following the line of the spine, cut through the center of the fish from one end to the other. Remove the top (dorsal) half of the fillet by letting your spoon and knife push it off the bone. Remove any bones that are still attached to the dorsal fillet.

Repeat with the bottom (belly) half of the fillet.

Removing any stuffings in the way, lift the tail and gently lift out the backbone. Discard.

Scrape away any bones from both halves of the bottom fillet. If you'd like, you can neatly reassemble the fillets and serve with the head; or simply divide the fillets among serving plates.

WHOLESOME

BAKES

I love the way that simple ingredients can come together into little delights that make everyday moments worth celebrating. The smell of biscuits just out of the oven brings my whole family into the kitchen. A batch of shortbread cookies invites a reason to sit down with a friend over a cup of tea. A lightly sweet day cake becomes the way I say thanks to a neighbor.

In my home, desserts are centered on of-the-moment cravings using the ingredients we already have in our pantry. These recipes can be made without specialty equipment or far-flung pastry ingredients, and come together with minimal prep. Because we rely on nutritious whole-grain flours and less sugar than you'd typically find in baked goods, these treats are designed to be enjoyed every day. Maple-sweetened cornbread can start the morning off right alongside a plate of fried eggs or accompany a pot of black-eyed peas for dinner. A slice of sweet potato loaf offers a pause between meetings. When celebrations arrive, a simple sheet cake bakes in 15 minutes and is romantically stacked with layers of fruit and freshly whipped cream.

Baking doesn't have to mean stressing over complicated projects or settling for a box of premade mix. Each of these from-scratch recipes will invite you to enjoy the process with ease. Go ahead and add a little sweetness to your day.

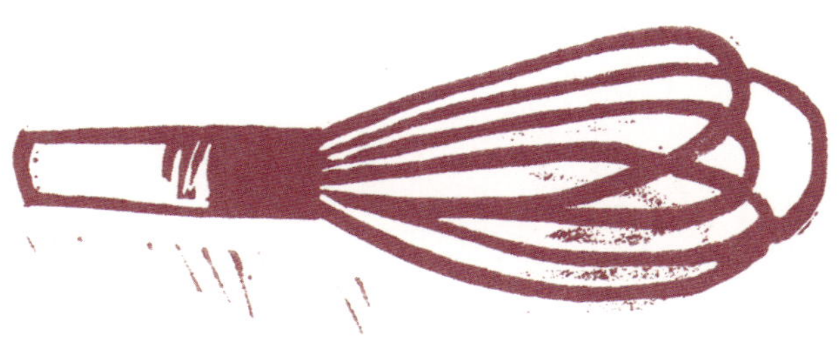

BAKED CARAMEL APPLES

Serves 3 to 6

This recipe is perfect when you're dreaming of pie but want something a bit simpler. Oven-caramelized apples make a beautiful dessert served alongside fresh whipped cream, or an indulgent breakfast over yogurt. When selecting apples for baking, look for crisp, tart varieties like Pink Lady. This technique also works nicely with pears or stone fruit.

Gluten-free

½ cup (105g) light brown sugar

3 tablespoons unsalted butter, cut into pieces

3 tablespoons water

1 teaspoon vanilla extract

3 small, crisp apples, halved and cored

¼ teaspoon ground cinnamon

Flaky sea salt, for sprinkling

Greek yogurt or Softly Whipped Cream (page 197), for serving

Preheat the oven to 425°F.

Scatter the brown sugar and butter into a large (at least 12-inch) cast-iron skillet or a 2-quart ceramic baking dish. Pour in the water and the vanilla. Arrange the apples, skin-side up, over the sugar mixture.

Bake until the apples are just tender when pierced with a paring knife, 15 to 20 minutes.

Remove the pan from the oven and place on a heat-safe surface. Use tongs to remove the apples, skin-side down, to a serving dish. Return the pan to the oven and continue to bake until the caramel sauce has reduced by about half and is bubbling furiously, another 8 to 10 minutes.

Return the pan to a heat-safe surface. Whisk the cinnamon into the caramel sauce until it's smooth. Let the sauce sit for 5 minutes to cool and thicken (the longer it sits, the thicker it gets).

Drizzle the caramel over the apples and sprinkle generously with flaky sea salt. Serve the apples with a big dollop of yogurt or whipped cream. Best eaten immediately.

*HOW TO BAKE BETTER**

Eating well every day doesn't mean cutting out baked goods and sweets, but it does mean being more thoughtful about what goes into them. Sweets from a package (or even a great bakery) tend to be loaded up with more sugar than you'd bake with at home, and typically use only highly refined flours. That combination makes them delicious to eat but hard to fill up on. Cue the vicious cycle of bellyaches. Here are the guidelines I bake by to bake better:

USE LESS SUGAR

I've found that most recipes for desserts can have the amount of sugar cut back by a third and still be plenty sweet. Keep in mind that adjusting sugar can impact the tenderness of your finished bake—all of the following recipes have been tested to be deliciously soft and a little less sweet.

EMBRACE NATURAL SWEETNESS

Baking with minimally processed sweeteners like unbleached cane sugar, maple syrup, and honey is a great way to cut back on the amount of refined sugar you're using, or to swap it out altogether.

GO BEYOND ALL-PURPOSE

I like to bake primarily with whole wheat flour, which lends more fiber, nutrients, and a more complex flavor than refined white flour. (Sometimes 100% whole wheat bakes can be a little dry, but mixing with all-purpose flour strikes a nice balance of texture and flavor.) This is also a great opportunity to explore mixing in other alternative grains and flours, like cacao powder, rye, cornmeal, and buckwheat.

ADD MORE FAT, PROTEIN, OR FIBER

Adding extra whole foods to your baked goods makes them more filling and nourishing. Baking with yogurt adds protein; nuts, oats, shredded carrots, and even cooked sweet potatoes add fiber. As always, don't fear the fat. Rich, yellow egg yolks, whole milk, and grass-fed butter will infuse your treats with nutrition and help to keep you full.

*Healthier, easier, but always delicious.

CHEWY GRANOLA COOKIES

Makes about 24 cookies

These tiny sweet and salty cookies are "oatmeal-plus": Fold your favorite granola ingredients into the dough. You can try swapping out my mix-in choices for chopped chocolate, other nuts and seeds, raisins, or other small dried fruit.

Heaping ¾ cup (100g) rolled oats

⅓ cup (50g) finely chopped walnuts

⅓ cup (50g) finely chopped pecans

⅓ cup (50g) dried currants

5 tablespoons (50g) whole flaxseeds (golden or brown)

8 tablespoons (113g/1 stick) unsalted butter, melted and cooled

½ cup plus 2 tablespoons (130g) light brown sugar

1 egg

1 teaspoon vanilla extract

¾ cup (94g) whole wheat flour

½ teaspoon baking soda

½ teaspoon baking powder

1 teaspoon cinnamon or cardamom

¼ teaspoon sea salt

Flaky sea salt, for sprinkling

Preheat the oven to 350°F. Line two sheet pans with parchment paper.

In a small bowl, stir together the oats, walnuts, pecans, currants, and flaxseeds. Set aside.

In a medium bowl, whisk together the melted butter and brown sugar, breaking up any lumps. Whisk in the egg and vanilla until smooth. Sprinkle on the flour, baking soda, baking powder, cinnamon, and salt and whisk until just barely combined. Use a spatula to fold in the oat mixture.

Use two spoons to scoop out half the dough into 12 balls onto one of the prepared sheets, about 1 inch apart (they will spread).

Bake the cookies until the edges are lightly golden, 8 to 10 minutes. While the first pan is in the oven, scoop another 12 cookies for the second pan.

Remove the first pan from the oven and immediately top each cookie with a pinch of flaky sea salt. Put the second pan of cookies in the oven.

Let the salted cookies cool on the pan for 5 minutes, then transfer to a wire rack to cool completely. Once the first sheet pan is emptied and cooled, use it to bake the remaining cookies.

JAPANESE SWEET POTATO LOAF

Makes one 8½ by 4½-inch loaf

I like to bake a batch of sweet potatoes and store them in the fridge for adding to meals and for snacking—this is another great use for them. You can make this recipe with any variety of sweet potato, but I love the gentle flavor of a Japanese sweet potato (the ones with purple skin and white flesh) in this loaf. The whole wheat flour, eggs, and potato make a slice of this filling for breakfast or a daytime snack, but it's sweet enough to enjoy for dessert, too.

Olive oil, for the pan

1⅓ cups (263g) granulated cane sugar

Grated zest of 1 large orange (optional)

3 large eggs

7 tablespoons (90g) extra-virgin olive oil

¾ cup (215g) mashed Japanese sweet potato (from 1½ to 2 medium baked, see page 61)

1½ cups (188g) whole wheat flour

½ cup (68g) coarsely chopped toasted walnuts or pecans (optional)

1½ teaspoons sea salt

¾ teaspoon freshly grated nutmeg

¾ teaspoon baking powder

½ teaspoon baking soda

Grease an 8½ by 4½-inch loaf pan lightly with olive oil. Line with a piece of parchment paper along the longer sides, leaving at least 1 inch overhang on each side. Preheat the oven to 350°F.

In a large bowl, combine the sugar and orange zest (if using) and rub the zest into the sugar with your fingers until it's fragrant and slightly moistened. Add the eggs and whisk until smooth. Continuing to whisk, stream in the olive oil and mix until smooth. Whisk in the mashed sweet potato until well incorporated.

Sprinkle on the flour, nuts (if using), salt, nutmeg, baking powder, and baking soda, then use a spatula to fold the batter until combined. Scrape the batter into the prepared pan and smooth the top.

Bake until a cake tester inserted into the center comes out clean, 1 hour 10 minutes to 1 hour 20 minutes.

Let the loaf cool in the pan for at least 20 minutes before pulling out by the parchment sling and slicing.

WHOLE WHEAT YOGURT BISCUITS

Makes 6 biscuits

These biscuits are flaky and rich like a classic rolled biscuit, but the addition of whole wheat flour and whole-milk Greek yogurt yields a bake that's more filling and nutritious than its more refined cousins. If you want to serve these for dessert, split them and spoon Shortcake Strawberries and Softly Whipped Cream (page 197) on top.

8 tablespoons (115g/1 stick) cold unsalted butter, cut into ½-inch cubes

Scant 2 cups (240g) whole wheat flour, plus more for dusting

1 tablespoon baking powder

2½ teaspoons cane sugar

½ teaspoon sea salt

¼ teaspoon baking soda

Scant 1 cup (230g) whole-milk Greek yogurt (see Note)

1 egg, beaten

Flaky sea salt, for sprinkling

Turbinado sugar, for sprinkling

NOTE: **A Greek yogurt that's similar in texture to sour cream works best here. If yours is firmer, add a splash of milk to loosen it up.**

Place the cubed butter in the refrigerator and chill while you start the dough. Preheat the oven to 450°F. Line a sheet pan with parchment paper.

In a large bowl, whisk together the flour, baking powder, cane sugar, salt, and baking soda.

Toss in the butter cubes to just coat them in the flour mixture. Use your thumb and forefinger to press the cubes into thin shards. (They should be about 1½ inches across at the largest, with the edges thinner than the centers.)

Use your hands to make a well in the center of the mixture, then add the yogurt. Gently mix together with a fork into a loose and shaggy dough. Continue to mix until the yogurt is incorporated and there are no totally dry areas of flour mixture. The dough shouldn't be smooth, and there should be visible pieces of butter.

Lightly dust a work surface with flour, then dump out the dough. Gently press the dough together into a 5½-inch square about 1 inch thick.

Use a floured knife or a bench scraper to cut the dough square into quarters. Stack the quarters on top of each other, pressing in the edges as needed to incorporate drier areas of the dough. Use a rolling pin or your hands to press down the dough again to form a 5½-inch square. Repeat this step twice (for a total of 3 stacks-and-presses), which will help create flaky layers in the biscuit.

After your final stack-and-press, press out the dough further to make a 6 by 5-inch rectangle about 1 inch thick. Cut the rectangle in half the long way, then into thirds the short way to make 6 square biscuits.

Divide the biscuits evenly on the sheet pan. Brush the tops of each biscuit with beaten egg, then sprinkle with flaky sea salt and turbinado sugar.

Bake the biscuits until puffed and golden brown, 15 to 18 minutes.

Transfer the biscuits to a wire rack to cool for 10 minutes. Serve warm.

SHORTCAKE STRAWBERRIES

Makes about 1 cup

I love using frozen strawberries here: They hold their form and texture nicely through the cooking. For strawberry shortcake, layer these jammy berries with halved Whole Wheat Yogurt Biscuits (page 194) and Softly Whipped Cream (below).

Gluten-free, vegan

- 4 cups frozen whole strawberries (see Note)
- ⅓ cup cane sugar
- 3 tablespoons fresh lemon juice
- ½ teaspoon sea salt
- 1 tablespoon white or red vermouth (optional)

In a medium saucepan, combine the berries, sugar, lemon juice, and salt. Cook over medium heat, stirring occasionally until the berries have mostly thawed and the liquid is simmering, 3 to 5 minutes.

Increase the heat to medium-high and continue to cook, stirring often, until the strawberries have wilted and the rest of the mixture is thick enough that you can drag a spatula across the pot and liquid slowly oozes in to fill the bare spot, another 10 to 15 minutes.

If using, stir in the vermouth, then turn off the heat. Let the berries cool in the pot for 10 minutes. Transfer the mixture to a heatproof bowl to cool to room temperature, then serve.

NOTE: To make this with fresh strawberries, halve them and toss in a large bowl with the sugar. Let the fruit macerate in the sugar for at least 30 minutes or refrigerate, covered, overnight, before cooking. Fresh berries will soften more than frozen, yielding more of an even-textured jam, which is still delicious.

SOFTLY WHIPPED CREAM

Makes about 2 cups

In a large bowl, use a whisk to beat together **1 cup cold heavy cream** with **1 teaspoon vanilla extract**, **1 teaspoon maple syrup** (optional), and **a pinch of salt** until it forms soft peaks, about 2 minutes.

OLIVE OIL AND MATCHA DAY CAKE

Makes one 8- or 9-inch cake

I first made a matcha loaf cake in 2020 during the height of pandemic-induced lockdown. We were looking for a way to connect with Golde's customer community, and decided on a virtual baking event highlighting our matcha powder. I spent a few days recipe testing a version made with pantry essentials everyone would hopefully already have, since even one extra trip to the grocery store was a worrisome thing at that time. This version is made with olive oil and maple syrup, just like the original, but we've added in warming spices and lemon zest to mingle with the green tea flavor.

⅔ cup (133g) extra-virgin olive oil, plus more for the pan

⅔ cup (208g) maple syrup

⅓ cup (76g) whole milk, at room temperature

2 large eggs, at room temperature

1 tablespoon grated lemon zest (optional)

1 teaspoon vanilla extract

2 cups (250g) all-purpose flour

2 tablespoons matcha

1 teaspoon baking powder

¼ teaspoon sea salt

½ teaspoon ground cardamom or cinnamon

Preheat the oven to 350°F. Drizzle 2 teaspoons olive oil into an 8- or 9-inch metal cake pan (square or round) and use a pastry brush to spread it around, coating the pan evenly. Line the pan with a piece of parchment paper, leaving at least a 1-inch overhang.

In a large bowl, whisk together the maple syrup, the ⅔ cup (133g) olive oil, the milk, eggs, lemon zest (if using), and vanilla until smooth. In a medium bowl, whisk together the flour, matcha, baking powder, salt, and cardamom. Whisk the dry ingredients into the wet ingredients until just combined. Scrape into the prepared pan and smooth the top of the batter with a spatula.

Bake until a cake tester inserted into the center comes out clean and the cake pulls away from the edges of the pan, 35 to 40 minutes for an 8-inch pan; or 30 to 35 minutes for a 9-inch pan.

Let the cake cool in the pan for 10 minutes, then lift out by the parchment onto a wire rack. Let cool completely, then slice and serve.

SALTED BUTTER SESAME SHORTBREAD

Makes 24 cookies

These slice-and-bake shortbread are the ideal cookie to enjoy with a steaming cup of tea. Salted butter perfectly seasons the dough, and a splash of toasted sesame oil gives a nutty flavor that complements its sweetness. I like to keep a log of dough in the freezer to thaw for baking on demand.

15 tablespoons (210g) salted butter (see Note), at room temperature, cut into small pieces

½ cup (100g) cane sugar, plus 1 tablespoon for rolling the dough

1 teaspoon toasted sesame oil

2¼ cups plus 2 tablespoons (300g) all-purpose flour

3 tablespoons sesame seeds

½ teaspoon flaky sea salt

1 egg white, lightly beaten

NOTE: If using unsalted butter, add ½ teaspoon sea salt along with the butter.

In a large bowl, use a whisk to cream together the butter, ½ cup (100g) of the sugar, and the sesame oil until light and fluffy. Use a spatula to scrape down the sides of the bowl, then fold in the flour until combined.

Tear two large pieces of parchment paper and lay them on a work surface. Divide the dough in half, placing each half on the parchment. Fold the parchment over one piece of dough, then use your hands to gently roll it into a log about 2 inches in diameter. Repeat with the other half of the dough. Twist the edges of the parchment to seal the logs.

Place the wrapped logs in the refrigerator and let chill for at least 1 hour, or up to 3 days. (Alternatively, freeze for up to 3 months; thaw overnight in the refrigerator.)

When you're ready to bake, preheat the oven to 350°F. Line a sheet pan with parchment paper.

In a small bowl, use your fingers to mix together the sesame seeds, remaining 1 tablespoon sugar, and the flaky sea salt, breaking up the salt a bit. Sprinkle the mixture onto a large plate.

Unwrap one of the chilled dough logs. Use a pastry brush to coat the outside of the log with the beaten egg white. Roll the log in the sesame mixture until it's totally coated.

Slice the log into ½-inch-thick rounds, then arrange on the prepared sheet pan about 1 inch apart from each other.

Bake until lightly golden brown and slightly puffed, 12 to 15 minutes.

Let cool on the sheet pan for 5 minutes before transferring to a wire rack to cool completely.

While the first batch of cookies come out of the oven, coat the second log of dough with more egg and sesame seed mixture, slice, then bake.

APRICOT-CORNMEAL GALETTE

Makes 1 galette

Our first daughter was born in high summertime. We had a container of apricots from the farmstand on the counter that we'd bought just before her arrival, and they were growing sweeter by the day. Issey and I fashioned them into rustic little tarts that we ate the next morning with a dollop of yogurt. Now the taste of a summer apricot brings me right back to that sweet moment at home as a very new family.

Plums or peaches can be used in place of the apricots, depending on what you can get your hands on at the moment.

1 round Galette Dough (recipe follows)

1 pound apricots, halved, pitted, and thinly sliced

6 tablespoons (75g) cane sugar, plus more for sprinkling

3 tablespoons medium or finely ground cornmeal

2 tablespoons apple cider vinegar or lemon juice

½ teaspoon sea salt

All-purpose flour, for dusting

1 egg, beaten

Make and chill the galette dough as directed.

In a large bowl, stir together the apricots, sugar, cornmeal, vinegar, and salt. Let sit for 15 minutes or up to 1½ hours.

Dust a large piece of parchment paper lightly with flour. Remove the chilled dough round from the refrigerator and place on the parchment. Dust the dough lightly with flour. Roll out the dough into a round that's about ⅛ inch thick and 12 to 13 inches in diameter, flipping over the dough and dusting with more flour as needed to prevent sticking.

Transfer the parchment with the crust onto a sheet pan. Use a slotted spoon to scoop out the apricot filling (leaving excess liquid in the bowl) into the center of the dough, leaving a 2-inch border. Use a pastry brush to paint some beaten egg around the perimeter of exposed dough. Fold the edges of the dough over the filling toward the center to encase the filling.

Refrigerate the galette on the sheet pan for 20 minutes (or freeze for 10 minutes). Meanwhile, preheat the oven to 400°F.

Remove from the fridge and brush the exposed crust with more egg wash, then sprinkle with some sugar.

Bake until the crust is golden brown and the filling is bubbling, 40 to 50 minutes, rotating the pan front to back halfway through baking.

Let the galette cool on the pan for at least 20 minutes. Serve warm or at room temperature.

CONTINUED

GALETTE DOUGH

Makes enough for 2 galettes

3½ cups (438g) all-purpose flour, plus more for dusting

2 tablespoons cane sugar

1 teaspoon sea salt

10 ounces (282g/2½ sticks) cold unsalted butter, cut into ½-inch cubes

1 egg

¼ cup cold water, plus more as needed

This recipe makes 2 crusts. Whatever you don't need right away can be frozen for the next time you want to make something.

In a large bowl, use your hands to mix together the flour, sugar, and salt. Toss in the butter to coat in the flour mixture. Rub and smash the butter between your fingers, until the mixture takes on a sandy texture with pieces of butter about the size of small peas (pick up a fistful and squeeze, it should hold its shape, then crumble apart).

Make a well in the center of the flour/butter mixture, then crack in the egg and add the water. Use a fork to gently beat together the egg and water, then combine the mixture into a very shaggy dough. Use your hands to gently knead the mixture once or twice until it forms a slightly more combined, but still shaggy, dough. If the mixture seems very dry, add more water by the teaspoon until it comes together.

Dust a work surface with a bit more flour and pour out the dough. Knead the dough together a few more times until there are no longer any dry bits of flour. Divide the dough in half (each half should be about 420g). Pat each half into a round that's about ½ inch thick. Wrap tightly in parchment paper. Refrigerate for at least 1½ hours (or up to 2 days) to let it rest and fully chill.

BROWN BUTTER BUCKWHEAT BROWNIES

Makes 12 large or 16 small brownies

Buckwheat flour is an earthy foil to rich chocolate in these brownies, which just so happen to be gluten-free. They get more fudgy as they sit—don't rush the cool time.

Gluten-free

- ¾ cup (150g) cane sugar
- ¼ cup plus 1 tablespoon (30g) cacao powder
- 14 tablespoons (197g) unsalted butter, cut into small pieces
- 2 eggs
- 1 egg yolk
- 1 teaspoon vanilla extract
- ½ cup (60g) buckwheat flour
- ½ teaspoon baking powder
- ¼ teaspoon sea salt

Preheat the oven to 375°F. Line an 8 by 8-inch metal cake pan with two long pieces of parchment paper, leaving an overhang on all four sides.

In a large bowl, whisk together the sugar and cacao powder.

In a medium saucepan or skillet, melt the butter over medium heat and let the butter continue to cook, whisking often, until it starts to smell nutty and goes a deeper golden brown in color, 6 to 8 minutes.

Immediately whisk the brown butter into the sugar mixture, making sure to scrape in all the browned bits stuck to the pan.

One at a time, whisk in the whole eggs and egg yolk. Whisk in the vanilla. The mixture should start out a little lumpy but go smooth as you continue to whisk.

Sprinkle the buckwheat flour, baking powder, and salt into the bowl, then whisk until the batter is smooth. Pour the batter into the prepared pan.

Bake until a cake tester inserted in the center comes out clean, 20 to 25 minutes.

For the best texture, let the brownies cool at room temperature for at least 2 hours, but 24 hours is best. Pull them out of the pan by the parchment and slice.

HONEY LEMON TART

Makes one 10-inch tart

This tart is an ode to the lemon bars of my childhood. By using a round pan, you can cut the bars into wedges rather than squares, so every slice gets a generous bit of crust (an answer to the eternal quest for a corner piece). I use honey in place of cane sugar in the filling, which lends a delicate floral sweetness. A mix of rye and all-purpose flour in the crust offers a nutty, textured contrast with the sweet filling.

CRUST

1¼ cups (156g) all-purpose flour

¾ cup (100g) rye flour

⅓ cup (67g) granulated cane sugar

¾ teaspoons sea salt

11 tablespoons (154g) unsalted butter, cut into small pieces, softened

FILLING

4 eggs, at room temperature

½ cup (168g) honey

4 teaspoons grated lemon zest (from about 3 lemons)

Pinch of sea salt

Scant ⅔ cup (150g) fresh lemon juice (from about 3 lemons)

2 tablespoons all-purpose flour

4 teaspoons medium or fine-grind cornmeal

Powdered sugar, for dusting

Make the crust: In a large bowl, whisk together both flours, the granulated sugar, and salt. Add the butter and use your fingers to massage it into the flour mixture until well incorporated (the dough should feel like moistened sand and hold its shape when you squeeze it in your hand).

Press the dough into a 10-inch pie pan, building it about 1 inch up the sides of the pan. Use a fork to prick all over the base of dough. Place the pan in the freezer for 20 minutes.

While it's chilling, preheat the oven to 400°F.

Bake the crust until slightly puffed and lightly golden, 14 to 17 minutes. If the crust slips down at all, use a measuring cup to gently press it up immediately after removing from the oven.

Let cool for at least 15 minutes while you prepare the filling. Reduce the oven temperature to 350°F.

Make the filling: In a large bowl, whisk together the eggs, honey, lemon zest, and salt until smooth. While whisking, slowly pour in the lemon juice and continue to beat until smooth. Whisk in the flour and cornmeal until combined.

Place the pan with the crust on a sheet pan—this will catch any drips and make it easier to remove from the oven. Pour the filling into the crust (hold back on some if the crust looks well filled).

Return to the oven and bake until the filling is just set (give the pan a little shake, it shouldn't jiggle much), 20 to 25 minutes.

Allow the tart to cool completely, at least 30 minutes, at room temperature. Dust with powdered sugar if you'd like just prior to serving, then slice into wedges and serve.

RUBY'S CHOCOLATE MUFFINS

Makes 12 muffins

These whole wheat muffins are just lightly sweetened with brown sugar. When I made these for the first time, my elder daughter instantly declared them her new favorite recipe. I like using raw, less-processed cacao powder when baking—it can be found in many supermarkets and natural foods stores.

Olive oil, for the pan

Scant ¾ cup (175g) whole milk

½ cup (100g) olive oil

Scant ½ cup (100g) light brown sugar

2 eggs

2 teaspoons vanilla extract

1½ cups (190g) whole wheat flour

½ cup (50g) cacao powder

2 teaspoons baking powder

¼ teaspoon baking soda

¼ teaspoon sea salt

Turbinado sugar (optional), for sprinkling

Preheat the oven to 375°F. Grease 12 cups of a standard muffin tin with olive oil or line with paper liners.

In a large bowl, whisk together the milk, olive oil, brown sugar, eggs, and vanilla until smooth.

In a medium bowl, whisk together the flour, cacao powder, baking powder, baking soda, and salt until there are no lumps.

Add the dry ingredients to the wet and use a whisk to gently fold them together until combined (the batter will be thick).

Divide evenly over the 12 cups, about 3 tablespoons per cup. Sprinkle each muffin with a bit of turbinado sugar (if using).

Bake until the muffins are puffed and a cake tester inserted into the center comes out clean, 15 to 20 minutes.

Let the muffins cool for 5 minutes before removing from the tin.

CARROT CAKE WITH LEMON TURMERIC ICING

Makes one 8½ by 4½-inch loaf

I love carrot cake because it's designed to be loaded up with veg and nuts. My favorite is just sweet enough, and swaps a classic thick frosting for a zingy golden icing. The loaf format makes this bake a little more casual than a multitiered slice, encouraging us all to have a little more carrot cake in our lives.

CAKE

10 tablespoons (140g) unsalted butter

¾ cup plus 1 tablespoon (165g) light brown sugar

3 eggs, at room temperature

1 teaspoon vanilla extract

1⅔ cups (200g) all-purpose flour

1 teaspoon ground cinnamon

½ teaspoon sea salt

1 teaspoon baking powder

¼ teaspoon baking soda

¼ teaspoon freshly grated nutmeg

3 medium carrots, scrubbed, trimmed, and coarsely grated (about 2 cups/200g)

¾ cup (100g) finely chopped walnuts or pecans

¼ cup (35g) raisins

ICING

4 ounces (113g) cream cheese, at room temperature

4 tablespoons (55g) unsalted butter, at room temperature

1 teaspoon grated lemon zest

¼ teaspoon sea salt

½ cup (56g) powdered sugar

½ teaspoon ground turmeric

2 tablespoons fresh lemon juice

For the cake: Preheat the oven to 350°F.

Melt the butter in a medium pot on the stove over medium-low heat. Turn off the heat. Scoop out 1 tablespoon and use it to grease an 8½ by 4½-inch loaf pan. Line the pan with a sheet of parchment paper along the longer sides, leaving at least 1 inch overhang.

Pour the rest of the melted butter into a large bowl. Use a whisk to beat in the brown sugar until the sugar has dissolved. Beat in the eggs and the vanilla until smooth.

In a small bowl, whisk together the flour, cinnamon, salt, baking powder, baking soda, and nutmeg.

Use a spatula to fold the dry mixture into the wet mixture until just barely incorporated (there should be streaks of flour). Fold in the carrots, walnuts, and raisins until just combined (the batter will be thick). Scrape the batter into the prepared pan and smooth the top with the spatula.

Bake until a cake tester inserted into the center comes out clean, 55 to 65 minutes.

Let the cake cool in the pan for 20 minutes, then pull it out by the parchment sling onto a rack to cool completely.

For the icing: In a bowl, combine the cream cheese, butter, lemon zest, and salt and use a whisk to beat until very smooth. Slowly beat in the powdered sugar and turmeric until light and creamy in texture and yellow in color. Slowly whisk in the lemon juice until the mixture is looser and drizzle-friendly.

Remove the parchment from the cooled cake and set it on the wire rack, over a sheet pan to catch drips. Spoon the icing over the cake to coat the top, letting it naturally drip down the sides. Refrigerate for at least 1 hour to let the icing set a bit, or serve immediately, using a serrated knife to cut thick slices.

SWEET ROSEMARY CORNBREAD

Makes one 10-inch round cornbread

A true Southern-style cornbread batter's cornmeal base is important for the slightly nubby texture (using wheat flour creates something closer to a corn-flavored cake). It's also baked in a preheated cast-iron skillet for crisp, golden-edged crust. Traditionally, cornbread doesn't use any sweetener or other flavorings, but a touch of maple syrup and rosemary adds a beautiful flavor without turning this into dessert. Greek yogurt and olive oil give the bread an extra-moist crumb *and* filling protein and fat. Cornbread is best served hot and fresh out of the oven, so make this one just before you plan to serve it.

½ cup (100g) extra-virgin olive oil

2 cups (304g) fine or medium cornmeal

2 teaspoons dried rosemary, rubbed to crush, or 2 tablespoons finely chopped fresh rosemary

2 teaspoons baking powder

½ teaspoon sea salt

1 cup (230g) whole-milk Greek yogurt, at room temperature

7 tablespoons (100g) water

¼ cup (84g) maple syrup

2 eggs, at room temperature

Pour the olive oil into a 10-inch cast-iron skillet, then place in the middle rack of the oven. Preheat the oven with the oil-filled skillet inside to 400°F.

In a large bowl, whisk together the cornmeal, rosemary, baking powder, and salt. In a medium bowl, whisk together the yogurt, water, maple syrup, and eggs until smooth. Whisk the yogurt mixture into the cornmeal mixture.

Remove the hot skillet from the oven and place on a heat-safe surface, like your stovetop. Quickly and carefully pour the hot oil from the skillet into the batter. Whisk until the batter is smooth, and then pour the batter into the hot skillet (it should make a sizzling sound).

Bake until the cornbread is golden at the edges and a cake tester inserted in the center comes out clean, 22 to 25 minutes.

Let cool slightly, then slice and serve warm.

NOTE: This cornbread uses a technique I learned from Edna Lewis's book *A Taste of Country Cooking*: pouring hot oil directly into the batter itself. I've found that using hot oil in the batter delivers a crisper texture and sweeter flavor. Be sure to move quickly—the pan should still be very hot when you pour the batter in to bake. If you don't hear the sizzle, you can still go ahead with baking it, but the cornbread may stick to the bottom of the pan—use a flexible spatula to help remove it.

CELEBRATION CAKE

Makes one 11 by 4-inch layer cake; serves 8 to 10

Every time we have a birthday celebration in the family, we make this cake. A simple batter baked in a sheet pan cooks in 15 minutes, and then transforms into a many-layer cake with a bit of jam, whipped cream, and joyful assembly. It's dramatically lower in sugar than any birthday cake you can buy, and the use of seasonal fruit jam makes each version feel distinctly special to the moment you're making it in. Four tiers of cake feels much fussier than it really is—the frosting technique is organic, but lovely—and serves as a present in its own right.

CAKE

Softened butter and flour, for the pan

2 sticks (226g) unsalted butter, at room temperature

1¼ cups (250g) cane sugar

4 eggs, at room temperature

1 cup (230g) whole milk, at room temperature

2 teaspoons vanilla extract

2 cups (250g) all-purpose flour

1 tablespoon baking powder

¾ teaspoon sea salt

ASSEMBLY

1 cup (230g) heavy cream

1 teaspoon cane sugar

1 teaspoon vanilla extract, or ½ teaspoon almond or lemon extract

Pinch of sea salt

¾ cup Skillet Jam (page 68), plus more for topping if desired

Fresh fruit, preferably the same variety used in the jam, for topping

For the cake: Preheat the oven to 350°F. Grease a half-sheet pan (18 by 13 inches) with butter, then line with a sheet of parchment. Butter the parchment, then sprinkle a couple spoonfuls of flour into the pan. Shake the pan around to evenly coat with flour, then tap out the excess.

In a large bowl, use a whisk to vigorously beat together the butter and sugar until light and fluffy. Scrape down the bowl.

Whisk in the eggs, one at a time, scraping down the bowl after each addition. Whisk in the milk and vanilla until smooth.

Sprinkle in the flour, baking powder, and salt. Use the whisk and a folding motion to gently incorporate the dry ingredients until mostly combined, then switch to a spatula and gently fold to combine until there are no streaks of flour.

Scrape the batter into the prepared pan, spreading with the spatula as needed to fill the area.

Bake the cake until it's starting to pull away from the edges of the pan, springs back when lightly tapped, and a cake tester inserted into the center comes out with a few moist crumbs, 15 to 20 minutes.

Let the cake cool in the pan until it's no longer too hot to handle. Once the cake has cooled slightly, flip it out onto a wire rack. Peel off the parchment and let the cake cool completely.

To assemble the cake: In a large bowl, use a whisk to beat together the heavy cream, sugar, vanilla, and salt until it forms stiff peaks, or beat with an electric mixer on medium speed for 3 to 5 minutes (see Note, page 216). Refrigerate while you assemble the cake.

CONTINUED

NOTE: **I like my whipped cream beaten into stiff peaks (nearly "butter," as a chef and farmer friend of mine chides). This is usually a matter of preference, but for this cake it's a must.**

When the cake is cool, trim the edges to make a perfect rectangle. Slice the cake in half lengthwise and crosswise (you should have 4 pieces each measuring about 11 by 8 inches). Place one piece of the cake on a serving plate. Use a spatula to spread ¼ cup of the jam over the surface of the layer. Place another layer of cake on top, then repeat with another ¼ cup of the jam. Repeat with remaining cake and jam, leaving the final layer of cake empty. At this point, you can leave the cake at room temperature for up to 2 hours.

When you're ready to serve the cake, top with big dollops of the whipped cream and spread to the edges. Top the cream with fresh fruit and a few more dollops of jam if using. Best enjoyed immediately.

Variations

You can play with the flavor combinations of fruit jam and whipped cream depending on the season. A few of my favorites:

Plum jam + whipped cream with almond extract

Raspberry jam + whipped cream with lemon extract

Strawberry jam + whipped cream with vanilla extract

RESOURCES

BULK SUPPLIERS FOR QUALITY PANTRY GOODS

Farmer Ground Flour

Freshly stone-ground New York flour
farmergroundflour.com

Golde

Matcha powder and more superfood blends
golde.co

Gustiamo

My favorite sea salt (Trapani Sale) and other Italian imports
gustiamo.com

The Rice Factory

Japanese-grown rice, freshly polished to order in the United States
trf-ny.com

Séka Hills

California olive oil, grown and harvested by the Yocha Dehe Wintun Nation
sekahills.com

FINDING LOCAL FOOD

Farmers' Market, Farm Store, or CSA Program

Look via the USDA Local Food Directories.
usdalocalfoodportal.com

Food Co-op

Grocery Story runs a helpful directory on their website.
grocerystory.coop/food-co-op-directory

BIBLIOGRAPHY

Bhardwaj, R.L., A. Parashar, H.P. Parewa, L. Vyas. "An Alarming Decline in the Nutritional Quality of Foods: The Biggest Challenge for Future Generations' Health." *Foods 13,* no. 6 (2024): 877.

"Food Co-ops." Cooperatives for a Better World, betterworld.coop/sectors/sector-food.

Hill, Holly. "Food Miles: Background and Marketing." *ATTRA* (2008). attra.ncat.org/publication/food-miles-background-and-marketing.

ACKNOWLEDGMENTS

To my coauthor, Rebecca, you have made this book richer, more resilient, and all the more dear in my heart. Thank you for continuing to rally alongside me as I pushed to make this book as deep and as true as possible. And thank you for teaching this very insular person that there is so much to benefit from good partnership.

To my agent, Kitty Cowles, thank you for your vision, your confidence, and your inspiring presence.

To my editor, Cristina Garces, what a treasure it's been to work alongside you. Thank you for instilling your trust in my voice. Emma Campion, our designer: Thank you for sticking by my vision and putting up with my many particularities. What a beautiful book this is. Many thanks to the entire Ten Speed Press team for all your hard work putting this book together.

Our outrageously phenomenal photo team, Dane, Jane, Pearl, Katerina, Allie, and Jamaica: Working together in our home was truly one of the most delightful experiences of my life. Thank you for being so gracious, so adaptable, and so genuinely fun to work alongside. Many thanks to Overlook Farms, Blue Star Farm, and MX Morningstar for your beautiful eggs and produce. Tom and Nina, thank you for opening your front porch to us.

My endless gratitude to the friends and neighbors who tested (and retested) recipes. Special thanks to my family: Mom, Dad, Theresa, Mary, Kai, Louis, and Junko, thank you for standing beside me every step of the way.

Issey, as you taught me: "Commit to the thing, and it will commit itself to you." Thank you for being my original commitment, my family, and my partner in everything.

INDEX

Note: Page references in *italics* indicate photographs.

T

V

W

Y

Z

TEN SPEED PRESS
An imprint of the Crown Publishing Group
A division of Penguin Random House LLC
1745 Broadway
New York, NY 10019
tenspeed.com
penguinrandomhouse.com

Typefaces: Designova's Falcon Nuvo and Brian Willson's Broadsheet

Library of Congress Cataloging-in-Publication Data
Names: Wofford, Trinity Mouzon, 1993- author | Firkser, Rebecca author
Title: Eating at home: the nourishing practice of everyday cooking / by Trinity Mouzon Wofford with Rebecca Firkser.
Description: First edition. | New York, NY: Ten Speed Press, [2026] | Includes index.
Identifiers: LCCN 2025025771 (print) | LCCN 2025025772 (ebook) | ISBN 9780593836927 hardcover | ISBN 9780593836934 ebook
Subjects: LCSH: Cooking | LCGFT: Cookbooks
Classification: LCC TX714 .W625 2026 (print) | LCC TX714 (ebook) | DDC 641.5—dc23/eng/20250702
LC record available at https://lccn.loc.gov/2025025771
LC ebook record available at https://lccn.loc.gov/2025025772

Hardcover ISBN 978-0-593-83692-7
Ebook ISBN 978-0-593-83693-4

Editor: Cristina Garces | Editorial assistant: Kausaur Fahimuddin
Production editor: Liana Parry Faughnan
Designer: Emma Campion | Production designers: Mari Gill and Faith Hague
Production: Philip Leung
Food stylist: Pearl Jones | Food stylist assistant: Katerina Liakos
Prop stylist: Allie Ayers | Prop stylist assistant: Jamaica Gilmore
Digitech: Jane Gaspar
Recipe developers: Trinity Mouzon Wofford and Rebecca Firkser
Copy editor: Kate Slate | Proofreaders: Eldes Tran, Sigi Nacson, Hope Clarke, and Mark McCauslin
Indexer: Elizabeth Parson
Publicist: Kristin Casemore | Marketer: Andrea Portanova

Manufactured in China

10 9 8 7 6 5 4 3 2 1

First Edition

Photography by Dane Tashima
Illustrations by Issey Kobori
Cover design by Emma Campion